LIFE IN MEDIEVAL FRANCE

E. R. Chamberlin

SAPERE
BOOKS

LIFE IN MEDIEVAL FRANCE

Published by Sapere Books.

20 Windermere Drive, Leeds, England, LS17 7UZ,
United Kingdom

saperebooks.com

ISBN: 978-1-80055-531-0.

TABLE OF CONTENTS

INTRODUCTION: THE SHAPING OF FRANCE

Uniquely bestriding Europe, protected, not isolated by mountain ranges, its great rivers acting as highways, not as barriers, the land formed a natural meeting place of peoples. Long before it was a political whole, Strabo had been impressed by the potential for unity arising out of the riverine system which made a harmony out of variety. 'One is here tempted to believe in a direct act of Providence, seeing how the land is laid out — not at random but as though in accordance with some well-considered plan.' The Romans created a social harmony out of the variegated peoples already established in the land and constructed a military barrier along the Rhine and Danube to maintain it. In the front rank of the Germanic tribes pent behind that barrier, the Franks, Alemans and Burgundians pressed ceaselessly until the day the barrier broke and left Gaul helpless before them. They poured across, warred amongst themselves until, by the end of the fifth century, the Franks dominated on both sides of the Rhine. On Christmas Day, A.D. 496, their leader, Clovis, was baptised with 3,000 of his warriors, gaining thereby the formidable backing of the Christian Church, heir to what remained of Rome in Gaul. With that support Clovis' dynasty, the Merovingian, arose and gave a central control again to the land even while its members took to themselves some of the outward glory of Rome. Yet, though they might dress in purple and assume the styles of magistracy, they remained tribal chiefs, modifying the legacy of Rome according to the taste of a virile, still primitive people. The personal tie between chief and man took the place of the citizen's duty towards the state. The all-embracing Roman law disappeared as, following the German custom of trying each man according to the laws of his own tribe, a bewildering tangle of tribal codes appeared. Taxation, too, disappeared and, with it, the communal treasury: the king now granted benefices in return for services.

The office of Mayor of the Palace grew steadily in importance as the virility of the kings declined, and from that office grew the next dynasty. In A.D. 732 Charles Martel, acting theoretically in the name of the King, held and smashed the Arabs at the Battle of Poitiers. Already powerful in the land as Mayor of the Palace, the action won him enormous prestige which, transmitted to his children, brought one of them to the throne 19 years later. Then, in 768, Martel's grandson Charles came to the throne at the age of 26 and gave his name to the dynasty. For a generation, Charlemagne dominated not merely Francia but all Europe, bringing again, it seemed, the peace and stability that had vanished with Rome, infusing imperial power with Christian ideals when he received the crown of the Empire at the hands of the pope in A.D. 800. But the Empire had been revived too late or too soon and was largely the expression of his own immense personality, imposed upon a people incapable of sustaining it. In 843 his three grandsons divided the Empire between them and, in so doing, created France. Charles the Bald took the lands west of the Rhone, Louis the German took the region east of the Rhine and the brother Lothair, the titular Emperor, held Italy and the ambiguous area that lay between his brothers' kingdoms. As Lotharingia and, later, Lorraine it was to be endlessly disputed territory.

The year before the Treaty of Verdun thus geographically blocked out the land that was to be France, Charles and Louis had taken an oath of mutual protection and restraint. The East and West Franks had already grown so much apart that it was necessary to phrase the oath in what was virtually two languages. Each brother swore in the tongue of the other's new country, and that placed in the mouth of Louis the German was a language in the moment of transition — no longer Latin but not yet French. 'Pro Deo amur et pro Christian poblo et nostro commun salvament d'ist di en avant, in quant Deus savir et podir, me dunat, si salvarai eo cist meon fradre Karlo et in adiuda et in caduna cosa si cum om per dreit son fradre salvar dist...' There were to be more divisions, kingdoms were to be created and dissolved, but the language of the Oath of Strasbourg showed more clearly than any treaty that, henceforth, there were no longer West and East Franks but French and Germans.

Under a succession of increasingly feeble monarchs, the Carolingian dynasty gradually declined in power until it too was supplanted by a new and vigorous dynasty. The Capetians rose much as the Carolingians had done, gaining power and prestige as the result of a military action. Eudes, Count of Paris and Duke of the Île de France, defended Paris from the Normans when the King made a shameful peace with them. A descendant of Eudes — Hugh, nicknamed Capet — was elected king in 987 when the last Carolingian died without an heir. But 'king' now was a hollow title, the feudalism that had developed since the time of Charlemagne robbing the monarch of all effective power outside his own feudal domain. The first Capetians held, in their own right, an area little larger in size than a modern *départemente* — but the Île de France which formed its heart was in a vital position. The early Capetians might have appeared as dwarfs in the robes of giants. But their pretensions, ludicrous though they were without power to back them up, kept alive the sacred rights of the monarch which, in the twelfth century, were used to make France a nation.

During the long minority of the kings, the land itself acted as regent. The lack of major physical barriers alone prevented the components of West Francia from crystallising into sovereign states after the collapse of the Carolingian Empire. But the vast size of the country encouraged the growth of local lords, monarch in their locality in all save name. As late as the fifteenth century the section of France known as Burgundy could ally itself with the English King against the King of France as though it were making an alliance of two sovereign states against a third. A Burgundian, a Provençal or a Norman felt no particular affinity with the inhabitants of the area around Paris, the Île de France, from which the whole country eventually took its name.

Across the Channel, the accident of geography gave to the formative period of the English nation a framework denied that of the French. By the end of the ninth century, Alfred the Great had provided a persona for the otherwise inchoate national identity contained within the constant boundary of the sea. The Danish attempt to transcend that boundary was short-lived and Canute's Empire fell into its natural, geographic divisions after his death. Thereafter, though the crown of England was constantly in dispute, it was the crown of the whole country which was the prize, not the crowns of sections. A complete unit fell into the hands of the Conqueror and, for 400 years thereafter, his descendants, pursuing the grand design of an Anglo-French Empire, were able to draw upon resources in France greater at times than those possessed by the titular King of France.

To the political and geographical difficulties of isolating 'France' in its early centuries is added the cultural. The land was the wellspring of those institutions which made of nationalism a meaningless word in Europe for centuries. Feudalism, the dominant social organisation for over 500 years, was forged north of the Loire and, with chivalry, took its technical language from French speech, its characteristics from French *mores*. Monasticism, refashioned in Burgundy in the tenth century, deliberately strove to establish a standard pattern throughout Europe. A man was a Benedictine first and an Englishman, Frenchman or German as a very poor second; the abbot looked to the pope, not to the bishop, as his immediate superior. The schools and universities born of the intellectual renaissance of the twelfth century drew the web even tighter. Paris, Chartres and Orleans might be the centres of learning but their masters were drawn from all over Europe, so great was their attraction, and students would return to their own countries to disseminate the learning achieved in France. The very vitality of French culture blurred any nationalism that might have emerged. War was to achieve what culture could not. It was in the bitter humiliation of the years following Agincourt that the concept of 'France' became realised, centuries after the *Chanson de Roland* broached the idea of an entity superior to its parts. Agincourt was duly emblazoned in English annals but a generation afterwards, at Castillon in 1453, geography triumphed over race, the English were expelled and the two countries began their separate paths.

The twelfth century forms the central point of French history in a far more real sense than the accidental fact that it is the mid-point of the arbitrarily defined 'Middle Ages'. In that century venerable institutions flowered and died while new ones were born whose influences would reach far into the future. Feudalism and chivalry achieved then their final form and all that came after was a long decay; at the same time the universities came into being, together with the town as a political entity. Art flourished with learning, breaking the forms into which it had been clamped for centuries. The dynamism of the monastery fell away, its energy transferred to the cathedral. But, above all, France then began to know itself as a nation. The Albigensian Crusade in the first decades of the century brutally destroyed the glowing civilisation of the south when it dragged Provence, the too-distinct daughter of Rome, into the ambit of Paris, but it established the principle that France was superior to its provinces. And in 1214 the Battle of Bouvines, which began the prising of the English grip from the land, marked the open entry of the monarch upon the national stage after two centuries of covert preparation. The twelfth century is a kind of peak from which is visible that road which started at Verdun and ended at Castillon.

1: RURAL SOCIETY

The Feudal Lord

From north, east and south invaders passed into the still inchoate nation, inlets of a vast sea which thrust into the heart of the land now that the breakwaters were gone. The artificial unity imposed upon the land by the great Frankish Emperor had collapsed and each man looked to his own. The Huns came: lightly armed horsemen on incredibly agile mounts, sweeping out of the endless plains of the east to penetrate as far as Provence. They stopped there, hesitated, then flooded back to found that nation which became known as Hungary. Other invaders, no less destructive, found the land attractive so that, coming as robbers, they stayed as farmers. The Norsemen, skilled in seamanship and murder, used their long narrow ships as river craft to commute between settlements. They assaulted Paris, brought destruction even into Burgundy before receding in their turn to found a nation — Normandy, which was to exist co-equal with France until the thirteenth century. The ancient race on the North African shore crossed the Mediterranean to settle in Spain and parts of the land that was no longer Gaul but was not yet France. The wild predators of Europe emerged again from the primeval forests to prey upon man and animal, destroying the great estates. The land was sparsely populated, for famine, in this ninth century after Christ, was the norm with the total breakdown of communications. Society withdrew into itself, formed tiny islands protected by wooden walls. The natural horizon was the limits of the small clearing in the forest or cultivated area in the plain. The trackway that joined one to another was used, for the most part, only by men intent upon ill-will. The virtuous and the sensible man stayed in his village. Even 300 years later an abbot on Church affairs could describe his journey from Paris to Toulouse as though it were a journey through enemy country at time of war. 'I conjure you, my brethren, to pray to God and the Blessed Virgin for me. May They show me the grace of helping me back, safe and sound, to Paris.'

Yet, because society rarely regresses totally, the process of fragmentation stopped at its basic unit, the family and its associates. A man constructs a building a little larger, a little stronger than the huts of his neighbours: it cannot compare with the great stone castles of the succeeding centuries, for it consists simply of a wooden building on a mound of earth, surrounded by the ditch from which the earth was dug, and a wooden palisade. But it offers protection from casual marauders and, as a good neighbour should, he shares that protection with those who have not the means to build their own. This is, indeed, enjoined by the law, for Charlemagne, in those days which are now a legend, had decreed that all free men should choose a lord. His laws had never been rescinded, even though they had no force and men now acted solely in self-preservation. The free men, the retainers, form a natural bodyguard around their leader, protecting the little settlement of wood and banked earth that is the core of their world. Their numbers grow: sometimes their lord and his settlement will absorb another, sometimes they will be absorbed in a larger. Soon the area controlled by a settlement becomes larger than can be conveniently administered by one man; soon, too, the lord finds it necessary to bind his fighting men to him and therefore he grants land to them in return for their vow of loyalty. The vow is freely given for only under his strong arm is there peace and a little safety.

The *chansons de geste*, prime witnesses for this period of anarchy, return again and again to the theme that a man alone is a man destroyed, that unity is the only possible safeguard. But that unity utterly depends upon the fact that the bond between a man and his vassal is stronger than any human emotion and can outlast the conditions which created it, totally independent of fear or love or hatred or cupidity. Bernier, vassal of Raoul of Cambrai, hears that his mother has been murdered, with attendant atrocities, by his lord. Raoul humiliates him, mocks the very tie that binds them, but Bernier can do nothing but stand with limp hands. The act of homage that he has made has created an artificial force stronger than the natural force that links him to his mother. He has only one remedy — to abandon Raoul — and this he does but it is heinous enough. The true vassal would have continued not merely to serve Raoul, but to serve him with active love, the memory of his murdered mother an irrelevancy. Similarly, Aymon finds that his four beloved sons are in rebellion against his suzerain, the King who is overlord both of himself and his sons. It seems for a moment that his human love will overcome the superhuman loyalty demanded of him: that, at the very least, he will stand aside from this conflict in which he can only be the loser. But a councillor urges on him that even the tacit countenancing of his sons' rebellion against his suzerain would be actively to betray that suzerain, and so he declares himself their enemy. Bernier and Aymon are the ideal vassals, little more than poetic fictions woven around the men of the heroic age by minstrels living much later. But even in the cold, modern world fact sometimes substantiated poetry. Henry II of England, having Louis VII at his mercy, found himself unable to lay siege to his suzerain and marched away — albeit to the mockery of practical politicians. For 'loyalty', alike to a monarch in his own right as to a penniless lordling, means nothing more nor less than the upholding of that which is lawful. Without this law, the society painfully constructed from the fragments of anarchy will crumble.

The precise definition of feudalism has permanently eluded jurists and sociologists alike, for such a definition would have to include the whole range of human contact with fellow-humans. In the twentieth century, the strands of a citizen's corporate life can be separated clearly enough. Here he is employer or employee; there he is tax-payer or ratepayer, criminal or judge, consumer or producer — each of his manifold activities capable of definition and all contained within a body of precise laws whose whole purpose is to define the rights and duties of each citizen in relationship to his fellows. And above all a vast and impartial authority, the central government, knits the society into a whole. A feudal relationship is all-embracing and, by that fact, creates a microcosm. The exigencies of daily life force intercourse with the other microcosms but the independent life of the nucleus is guarded to the death. Speaking of the military system of France which was based upon scores of independent castles, Viollet-le-Duc observed that, 'Had feudalism been only united, it is certain that no system was so well calculated to arrest the progress of an invasion as this sub-division of the defence.' But, by the nature of feudalism, unity outside the seigneuries was impossible. There were laws, gradually shaping themselves into a canon, but daily life for the great as well as the obscure was founded on custom and concrete example. The very rents and dues were known as 'customs': the bizarre symbolism which defined or accompanied their payments once had a definite, rational purpose. That purpose forgotten, the symbolism yet continued. So, in Paris, the apprentice baker at the end of his time offered a bowl of nuts and cakes to the master who emptied the bowl and dashed it against the wall. Why? No man can now say except that it always had been done and therefore always must be done.

The only complete contemporary canon of feudalism as practised in northern France is that which, paradoxically, was drawn up for the administering of an alien land. After the fall of Jerusalem to the Crusaders in 1099 Godfrey of Bouillon compiled the code known as the *Assises de Jérusalem*, transplanting to oriental soil that which had grown up north of the Loire. Godfrey refused to take the title of King of Jerusalem, on the grounds that he could not wear a crown of gold in a city where his Lord had worn a crown of thorns, but his brother and successor Baldwin was less scrupulous, presiding over a court of barons who bore such exotic titles as Prince of Galilee, Lord of Sidon, Count of Jaffa. Each held their lands immediately of the crown in a voluntary association which could be dissolved if either lord or vassal neglected his duties. The unique *Assises* bequeathed to feudalism as a whole the appearance of logical form which was foreign to it. Its final shape is that of a pyramid with the monarch at the peak and, below him, increasing in numbers as each decreased in importance, the rest of society, with the manor — the economic unit of land — as the foundation of the whole. Yet monarch and manor were each outside the system, although it was dependent on them. The monarch, as his power grew, sought only the destruction of the system; the manor predated the system and survived it, for it originated in the great Roman estates, the *latifundia*, and its practices ultimately contributed in no small part to the Revolution.

The origins of the system lay in that fusing of Latin and Teutonic characteristics which followed the Frankish invasion of Gaul. But, in the fusing, the components lost their racial characteristics, producing a totally new thing. Charlemagne gave the Frankish instinct for free but collective action the force of law, for only in this way could he hope to administer the vast territories of which he was titular head, only in this way could he obtain the soldiers needed in the absence of a standing army. 'Whoever possesses four manses must equip himself at his own cost and present himself to the host. He who possesses three shall unite with him who possesses only one and the second man shall aid the first so that he may serve for both.' The Emperor's intention was to secure the stability of the central authority by ensuring that an army powerful enough to enforce its decrees could be swiftly gathered. His weaker successors allowed the process to continue until it resulted in the fragmentation of authority. The substitution of land tenure as the basis of military service, in place of the personal duty of the primitive Frankish tribesman towards his chief, began the erosion of personal freedom. All Franks were free, by definition, but many Franks were poor, and a landless man slipped down the social scale until his position was indistinguishable from that of a slave. The battle of Fontanet, in which the grandsons of Charlemagne destroyed his empire in their rivalry, destroyed finally that distinction.

The system of granting benefices of land, partly as an administrative policy, partly to retain the loyalty of followers, resulted in a permanent devolution of authority. The more a man received, the more powerful he became: his value and his price increased together and therefore the benefices granted for additional services were correspondingly larger. Beside these great vassals the monarch became a shadow. In 1016 a chronicler records: 'The king has now nothing save his title and his crown… he is not capable of defending either his bishops or his subjects. And therefore', the writer adds ominously, 'we see them all betaking themselves with joined hands to serve the great. In this way they preserve peace.' The search for peace and protection was the key to the development of feudalism. For every small man who lost his lands to a larger by an act of violence, there were a dozen who voluntarily surrendered their lands in return for protection. And, if a man had no land, then he sold himself. The act of homage perfectly illustrated the relationship. The potential vassal placed his hands together in the attitude of supplication; the potential lord placed his own hands around them, controlling and protecting.

Homage was made only once in a lifetime: death alone could dissolve the tie. So important was that act that never was it performed by proxy, except at a very late date when the king absolved his vassals from the need to present themselves personally. But this absolution was granted with considerable misgiving: for all other men and over the greater period of time, it was considered vital that lord and vassal should come into physical contact with each other at this crucial moment of their lives. The swearing of fealty that followed was a formality, a Christian imposition upon an essentially pagan ceremony and, unlike homage, was frequently renewed for specific purposes and could be made by proxy. Then came the whole point of the ceremony, the investiture of the vassal with his fief either in the form of new lands or the return of his own to him. He was being granted stewardship over a portion of the earth's surface and received as symbol a sod of turf, an olive branch, a stone or whatever the local custom prescribed. There were some 98 varieties of investiture, emphasising the personal, local tie between the vassal and the lands over which he now was lord.

On reaching his majority the young nobleman looked to his suzerain or to the king for land. Unlike the rigid English system of primogeniture, in which the younger sons were virtually dispossessed upon their elder brother's succession, the French system made provision for all the members of the family. But the land-hunger still had to be assuaged and, if the lord could not grant more lands, then his suzerain might do so: and if the suzerain could not, then an ambitious man would not hesitate to look elsewhere. In this manner homage was debased and its whole object perverted. The man of several lords became a commonplace: owing service to each of them in return for his lands, he was placed in an embarrassing position should any of them ever go to war against the others. The oath sworn to each in effect cancelled itself, and the vassal chose to serve a particular lord on the grounds of purest expediency — provided he was able to find an accommodating cleric who would release him from his vow. The Bishop of Chartres thus released a knight from his oath of fealty to William the Conqueror on the grounds that the oath conflicted with earlier engagements, 'contracted towards his lawful lords by right of birth'. As the system was beginning to creak, attempts were made to prop it up by the introduction, in the eleventh century, of liege homage. The vassal was tacitly free to perform homage to any number of lords but he swore to serve one — usually the most powerful — before all the rest, becoming his liege man.

The relationship between lord and suzerain was delicately balanced. A powerful lord was strongly tempted by the existence of a weak suzerain to allow expediency to oust loyalty; a powerful suzerain could easily persuade himself that national good took precedence over feudal rights. In 1126 Louis the Fat was conducting a vigorous campaign against the Count of Auvergne. The Count was at the end of his resistance, when his lord, William of Aquitaine, arrived to help him. Under other circumstances William might have attacked Louis and argued the legality afterwards, but Louis was powerful as a monarch and formidable as a man and William thought it prudent to make his objections in the most respectful of terms. 'May the grandeur of the Royal Majesty not disdain to accept the homage and services of the Duke of Aquitaine — or to preserve his rights. Justice demands that he should do you service but he would also that you should be to him a just suzerain. The Count of Auvergne holds Auvergne of me even as I hold it of you.' And because Louis, though hard, was a just man but most of all because the ignoring of the hierarchy would have been to introduce a most dangerous precedent, Louis agreed to arbitration.

A century later and the Duke of Aquitaine was also the King of England, demonstrating to the full the unwieldiness of the system. In 1138 it had seemed that the kingdom of France was at last a reality when Eleanor, daughter of the last Duke of Aquitaine, married the young Louis VII, bringing with her the vast possessions of her father. But the tremendous possibility was thwarted by the most unstable of human emotions, sexual love. Eleanor was light-hearted to the point of frivolity, Louis was serious, dedicated. Their union, indeed, could almost have been that kind of symbol that their people held dear, for it was the unhappy marriage of north and south. Eleanor had been deeply influenced by her father's cultured court and was elegant, witty, pleasure-loving, while Louis' ponderous approach to life was admirably summed up in his remark to Walter Map concerning the luxuries of the English court. 'At the court of France we have only bread, wine — and gaiety.' Eleanor would have agreed with the first part of the proposition but emphatically not the last and, though she charmed her husband, yet was she unable to win him from his liking for prelates and the drearier aspects of monarchy. He took her with him on Crusade, although already the bitterness of their private life was spilling into public view. In Syria, so much nearer her heart than the cold northern capital of France, she abandoned what little remained of conventionality until in Antioch a violent scene between them culminated in her public arrest. The scandal could no longer be hidden or endured: ties of consanguinity were conveniently found and, in March of that year, 1152, they were divorced. The personal sorrow it caused Louis was as nothing to the political embarrassment that followed, when, just six months after the divorce, Eleanor married the dashing young Henry Plantagenet. He became King of England shortly afterwards and, adding the Duchy of Normandy to his Aquitaine possessions, became lord of territories greater in France than that possessed by the King of France. Henry, too, was well aware of the danger of breaking precedent and so was punctilious in observing formal homage to Louis as his suzerain. But the formality could not disguise the fact that, over a vast area of France, an almost unworkable situation had been created.

The inevitable clash came over the matter of the 'king's cases'. The monarch had the right to interfere in all those law-suits that touched the national interest: his lawyers deliberately left their definition ambiguous. In those fiefs where lord and suzerain were on good terms, the suits which could be defined as king's cases were limited on a common-sense basis. But in Aquitaine, where two national prides were involved, points of potential conflict were endless. Faction here existed as it existed throughout Europe. The smaller nobles and the *bourgeois* identified themselves with the English King for the sufficient reason that their superiors, preferring a distant to an immediate lord, identified themselves with the King of France. Each group sought to exploit its relationship with its lord as a weapon against the other, the smaller people in particular employing their right to appeal against the judgements of their lord in the courts of his suzerain in Paris. The situation introduced chaos into the territorial courts and violence into the streets. The English complained, with justice, that 'murders and thefts remain unpunished', for so soon as a man was condemned he appealed to the suzerain and the case was automatically suspended until the court in Paris had decided. The normal leisurely pace of an appeals court was slowed even further by the judges' knowledge that, in delaying a decision, they were hindering the officers of the English King. But, though the English could do nothing either to prevent or to accelerate the process of an appeal, they could and did make life intolerable for the appellants. The court in Paris was forced to devise methods for the protection of its appellants and violence was met with violence. There could be no resolution of the problem unless one of the contending parties abdicated its lawful rights — or was forced to abandon them. The opportunity came under the forceful Philip Augustus who, stretching his rights to the very limit, summoned John of England to account for his misdeeds before a court of his peers. John was summoned as Duke of Normandy and when it was protested that the Duke of Normandy could not come without the King of England, Philip's brisk reply summed up the whole impossible complexity of feudal relationship in an international context. 'What of that? It is well known that my vassal the Duke of Normandy acquired England by force. But if a subject obtains any accession of dignity shall his paramount lord therefore lose his rights?' John not unnaturally declined to attend and, being judged a felon vassal, his fiefs were confiscated.

With the loss of his fiefs, John lost his legal rights for the possession of land was the basis of society. From that possession arose the right to dispense justice and this right in turn supported all other rights, whether it were the minting of coin, the hanging of a malefactor or the giving of a woman in marriage. The passionate defence of the claim to dispense justice more than any other cause hindered the progress of the country towards unity. The weakest of the Carolingian monarchs had yet attempted to ensure that this vital weapon for the defence of society was wielded only by the head of the society, but this principle, as so much else, disappeared in the universal breakdown. Over 300 years passed between the last Carolingian capitulary, enacted in 882, and the first effective ordinance of a king of France, that of Louis VIII in 1223, and, even as the legislative authority of the king disappeared so did the judicative. Justice now was tied to the territorial courts. There was a gradation in the powers of the judges according to the formula of property qualification: barons and *châtelains* alone had the right to exercise *la haute justice*, that involving life or death. But even this right was frequently accompanied by macabre disputes between rival and equal lords as to the possessions of gallows rights. These rights had a definite cash value: the condemned man was sent into the next world as naked as he had come into this, all that he had possessed falling into the hands of his judge and executioner. The desire to administer justice was throughout coloured by this lively awareness of its financial side. It was common knowledge that a poor man had little chance to present his case because he could bring no gifts, but, more important than the casual windfalls of bribery, was the constant revenue to be obtained by the levying of fines for exemptions or derelictions of the innumerable customs.

The absolute authority of the lord in his domain was tempered by the fact that he did not sit personally in judgement but appointed his agents to do so. Their freedom to deliver a judgement adverse to his interests depended for the most part on their own courage and his personal concept of justice. No wide legal training was necessary to enable a man to sit in judgement in these territorial courts. The appeal to custom was considered adequate basis for a sentence, supplemented by the accused's right to trial by combat should the case be doubtful. The introduction of this barbaric system, following as it did the civilised principle of rules of evidence to which the Carolingian courts adhered, is the clearest possible indication of the total breakdown of law. The *Assises de Jérusalem* assumed as a matter of course that trial by combat was an integral part of the administering of justice. Two hundred years later the climate of opinion had changed, particularly regarding those cases in which guilt was self-evident. Beaumanoir, a jurist writing in the late thirteenth century, observes: 'It would be a hard thing that if one had killed my near relative in open day before many credible persons I should yet be compelled to fight in order to prove his death.' Once the right had been available to all free men but by his time, he implies, it was limited only to the nobility. Most prudent men, as well as all women and clerics, confided their cause to a champion who would defend it for money. The execution of justice was thereby frequently turned into a contest between mercenaries. It was not an overcrowded profession: in order to prevent the obvious abuse of a champion selling the case, the loser was liable to have his hand struck off. If an appellant wished to impeach the court of false judgement he was obliged to vanquish every member within a single day. Failing, he was subject to death; but, if he triumphed, every member of the court fell under that sentence and the court lost its power for ever.

The gradual change in public opinion observed by Beaumanoir was to lead not merely to the abolition of the system but to a real, if subtle, increase in royal power and a consequent reduction in feudal rights. Trial by combat was such an obvious gamble, benefiting no one save those who enjoyed mortal combat, that almost any rational system was preferable. Such a system was adumbrated when Philip Augustus, a devious and a far-seeing king, established royal courts of justice in 1190. His *baillis* and *sénéchaux*, officers with ambiguous powers and duties, ingeniously took advantage of the ill-defined spheres of feudal rights to extend the practice of a formal legal code. A generation later and another and perhaps greater king, Louis IX, extended the code and, by the force of his remarkable personality, made of it a living thing. Better known to history as Saint Louis, he combined a genuine personal sanctity with boundless physical and moral courage. Joinville, no mean judge of men, spoke of him with near hero-worship whether describing his exploits as crusader or as king. Louis abolished trial by combat throughout his own domains and, in observing the spirit as well as the letter of the law, was able to present an example to be copied rather than a weakness to be mocked. Joinville has left a vivid account of how this regal but humble man administered justice.

> Many a time it happened that in summer he would go and sit in the forest of Vincennes after Mass, lean against an oak and bid us sit round him. Then those who had business to transact

came to speak to him — without being hindered by ushers or any other people. He then asked with his own lips, 'Is there any one here who has a suit?' Then those who had rose, and he said, 'Be silent all of you, and you shall be heard one after another.' And when he saw anything to amend in the words which spoke for him, or in the words of those who spoke for others he himself corrected it with his own lips. In order to despatch the cases, I have often seen him come into the Paris gardens dressed in a camlet coat with an overcoat of woollen stuff without sleeves, a cloak of black taffeta fastened round his neck, neatly combed, having no cap but merely a hat with white peacock's feathers on his head. He had carpets for us to sit upon and all those who had business for him to settle stood round him, and he heard the various cases according to the fashion I have mentioned above in the wood of Vincennes.

This quiet, deceptively informal, little group of men on the lawn of the Paris gardens effected a revolution as radical as that achieved in the streets 500 years later.

The Peasant

It should be known that there are three conditions of men in this world. The first is that of gentleman and the second is that of such who are naturally free, being born of a free mother. All who have a right to be gentlemen are free but all who are free are not gentlemen. The third estate of men is that of such who are not free. But these are not all of one condition, for some are so subject to their lord that he may take all they have, alive or dead, and imprison them whenever he pleases being accountable to none but God; while others are treated more gently, from whom the lord can take nothing but customary payments although at their death all that they have escheats to him.

So wrote Philippe de Beaumanoir, himself a gentleman and therefore happy enough with the existing order of things. But he was also a jurist, fascinated if not appalled by the tangle of law and custom which was strangling society, and his *Les Coutumes du Beauvoisis*, written about 1283, was an attempt to chart a path through the jungle. He, as others before and after him, was only partially successful in his attempt to define who was free and why. Bondage, he thought, was the result of four main causes. Some had given themselves to the Church in an excess of piety; others had sold themselves from sheer necessity 'or to be defended from other lords or from certain hatreds that men had against them'. A man was free because his mother had been, but the exact extent of his freedom was dependent entirely upon custom. Even a serf could 'disavow' his lord, but disavowal implied the abandoning of his own lands and goods: he would set forth on his travels possessing only the clothes upon his back. Knowing no other trade but that of the land, the serf who disavowed would inevitably starve. The chartered towns might admit him entry but the right to work was carefully controlled. If he were caught wandering at large then he would run the certain risk of being imprisoned or even executed as a vagabond, for the 'man without a hearth' was a menace to society. Therefore he stayed on the land where he was born, no more — and no less — valuable than the beasts who shared his labour.

A century before Beaumanoir puzzled himself over the existence of slavery, Peter the Venerable, the great Abbot of Cluny, had protested with deep sincerity against this trade in the bodies of men whom Christ had redeemed from the slavery of sin. Yet, for every ecclesiastic who was made uncomfortable by this betrayal of the principles of Christianity, many more could argue as convincingly that it was a natural, indeed a divine, law. Laud of Angers was merely enunciating accepted principles when, in his charter of affranchisement, he stated that 'amongst men some shall be lords and some serfs in such a way that the lords shall tend to venerate and love God and the serfs shall tend to venerate and love their lords'. The presumed equation of God with a local landowner, of divine worship with servile homage, seems to have passed unnoticed. There was some academic debate as to whether an ecclesiastic serf was better off than the serf of a lay lord, and a papal bull laid down that it were shameful if he were not. But as a general principle the serfs of a monastery were fed on a lower scale than the monks and the Abbot of Mont St-Michel did not hesitate to levy a tax in exemption of his *jus primae noctis* on the marriage of a daughter of a serf, exactly as a lay lord would do.

The role of the serf was purely economic, a forced consumer in times of glut and a producer at all other times. His body was, by a legal fiction, capable of being divided and sold to different lords. Thus the lord of Chauvigny held the serf Jean Bernard 'whole and undivided together with a quarter of Martin Bernard: the other three parts of the said Martin belong to the abbot and his convent'. That which he possessed was deemed to have been lent to him for the discharge of his tasks and had to be returned on his death. In the higher ranks of society the return of a fief on the death of a vassal was a formality; the *mainmorte* of the serf was a reality. Cardinal Jacques de Vitry called those lords who exacted *mainmorte* 'robbers of the goods of the dead... vultures who feed upon corpses', but such strictures did little to eliminate the squalid wrangles over the few poor possessions of a dead serf. Theoretically, it was an anachronism, a survival from the days when the lord lent horses and arms to his retainers and reasonably expected them back at their death. In practice it became a death duty. The lord took the best of his tenant's beasts or moveable goods as heriot, while the priest took the best of what was left as mortuary. Reasonable theory was thus turned into a shameful practice which was exerted only on the defenceless. A powerful lord could resist the application of an anachronism that did not favour him, while the widow of a serf could do nothing but stand by and watch her means of livelihood taken from her. The abbey of St Ouen at Rouen, in a customary of 1291, thought it easier to list what could not be taken than what could be, and ended the list with the remark 'all other moveables go to my lord abbot'. The exaction of *mainmorte* was proof of the heir's servile status, and a great lay lord, Goswin of Cariniers, seeking to establish the servile status of one of his men, was not ashamed to claim that on the death of the man's female relative he had taken 'coats, skins, and such things as a poor woman ought to possess'. The right to corpse-bedding was a logical if repugnant aspect of *mainmorte*. In 1204 Innocent III thought it prudent to issue a warning to his legates in Provence that the clergy there should have great care in exacting this dubious right. Nevertheless, over 200 years later, a jurist of Cluny compiled an elaborate defence of this exaction in approved scholastic style, advancing and demolishing objections to the confiscating of a dead man's bed. It was just 'because it had been the custom from time immemorial' and therefore should continue. He and others like him did their work well for *mainmorte* continued as a source of revenue until the eighteenth century.

Mainmorte was the most glaring, because the most obviously unjust, of anachronisms, but most of the existing customs were based on no more substantial reasons. During the long night of anarchy the existence of the lord had been its own justification. In his strength alone was there protection, the great walls of his castle were the enfolding arms into which small men could withdraw. It was common sense that he should be free of the humdrum daily toil of producing food so that he could maintain the great work of defence. His weaker neighbours took on these tasks and were glad to do so. The tasks became associated with one class of society and continued as customary dues long after the return of social stability eliminated the only reason for the lord's existence. Once it could have been argued with justice that the landless man contributed to his own defence by supplying the lord with daily necessities, but now that voluntary act had been corrupted into slavery. Those seigneurial monopolies called *banalités* were working examples of the process. The most common ban was that of the mill. In a small and poor community the establishment of a water-mill was beyond the resources of the serfs. Its provision by the lord was therefore an act of charity; it was also just that he should retain a proportion of the milled grain as return for his investment. But the privilege insensibly developed into a tyranny as the economic value of the ban became evident. It became merely another means of extracting produce, for every serf in the domain was obliged to grind his corn only at the ban mill. In a scattered village the serf might have to carry his sacks of grain for three or four miles, even though a mill was on his doorstep. Arriving at the ban mill he would invariably have to wait, particularly if the harvest had been good or if drought lowered the level of the mill-pond so that the machinery idled. He could claim an exemption from the ban only after waiting for a specified time. At Marnes near St Cloud the serfs of the abbey were obliged to wait only for one day and night before being free to seek another mill. In other places a serf might wait anything from 36 hours to three days and nights. A similar process of corruption from public service to tyranny occurred with the ban ovens. The serf was obliged to have his bread baked in the lord's oven, regardless of the incompetence or dishonesty of the baker. The lord's officers protected his ban of both oven and mill by the destruction of all those erected privately.

Other *banalités* extended to the consumption of produce, particularly that of wine. Apart from the great vineyards, every man would have his vines in the form of either a patch or a trellis about his house. Production was unpredictable. In some years there would be barely sufficient wine for the producer while in other years there would be a glut. In a glut year the lord would publish his ban, declaring that for a certain specified period only the wine produced on his estates could be drunk. The taverners closed during these periods and the serf was forced to drink — or at least to pay for — a certain quantity of wine. When the quality of the wine was bad a kind of black market seems to have sprung up. During a law-suit between the monks of St Germain-des-Prés and their serfs over the sale of wine *ad bannum* a gentleman deposed that, finding the wine was bad, he attempted to obtain some from the local taverner but was refused. A commoner declared that he had been successful — but had purchased the wine secretly.

The serf's obligation to consume his lord's surplus produce well illustrates his role as a mobile extension of the land. Jurists again and again argued that the value gained by the lord in such cases was out of all proportion to the inconvenience suffered by the serf. But throughout rural society was evidenced the disproportion between energy expended and yield obtained — a result of the twin causes of a vast captive labour force and a deep suspicion of innovation. For centuries, the two-field system of cultivation resulted in a tremendous waste of energy in order to obtain the staple foods. Each field was divided into two parts and a system of cultivation adopted which entailed the ploughing of nine acres in order to obtain three acres of grain. The three-field system of rotation first appeared in the northern half of France and later spread throughout northern Europe. But, though this reduced the numbers of acres to be ploughed and increased the acreage of grain, the resultant reduction in soil fertility reduced the total possible yield. The principle of manuring was well known but the barriers imposed by multiple ownership and lack of transport made of it a rarity. The valuable product of the stables of the Archbishop of Rouen was thrown into the Seine because it could not be taken to his own, distant, fields.

The yield of seed, though higher than in antiquity, was still very low, a bushel of seed producing on average four bushels of grain compared with today's average European yield of 1 to 20. The method of sowing seed by broadcast further reduced the potential yield; and, even when it had germinated and ripened, triumphing over its natural enemies, the standing crop could be burned as a legitimate act of warfare or left to rot if plague decimated the potential harvesters. Wheat was the staple, the aristocrat of foods, so that a man's status could be judged by whether he ate wheaten bread. Barley cakes formed a basic diet of the poor, supplemented with oats. In the south the lack of animal oils was compensated adequately enough by the olive: in the north oils were extracted from every plant capable of yielding anything that was not actually nauseous. The great walnut groves along the Seine provided a wholesome source, supplemented by oils from rose hips and even, towards the end of the fourteenth century, from poppies. Beans, peas, lentils and vetch comprised the major non-cereal crops. Beans were used largely as a form of bread, while considerable ingenuity was expended on developing a wide variety of peas: those of Normandy were particularly favoured.

A little wheat, barley, peas and beans, flavoured with vegetable oil and washed down with a thin, sour wine — this was the staple of most people over the greater part of the country. There is small wonder that famine and plague appear as norms in the chronicles. The lack of preservatives made it impossible to save the yield of a fat year for the inevitable lean years. The lack of public works exaggerated the effects of natural disasters: catastrophic floods occurred again and again within the bounds of their potential control. And the total absence of co-operation ensured that each little community was dependent only upon its own small reserves. A man's responsibility ended at the boundaries of his own land, so that it was sufficient to drive a marauding animal into a neighbour's fields.

The structure of society, with virtually independent nobles at the top and a mass without rights at the bottom, ensured that he was called upon to contribute most who was capable of contributing least. 'What the peasant produces in a year the lord wastes in an hour' was a recurrent theme of such moralists as Jacques de Vitry, but more destructive than noble extravagance was noble independence. No lord contributed to the common good unless he very clearly received something in return. Some of his rights spilled over on to the free man who, at least, was taxed only to a clear specification. The serf was taxed *à merci*, his lord alone deciding how much and when he should pay. It was of a pattern with his daily life in which all his energy was at the disposal of his lord, variously though its product might be disguised as forced labour, rent, or local dues. Producing food for himself and his family was a by-product. The pattern varied greatly from place to place, depending upon the nature of the dominant crop, the humanity of the lord, but, above all, on local custom. The phrase 'since time immemorial' occurred again and again as explanation and sufficient justification of an existing situation. Insensibly, the burdens could increase until it was impossible for the serf to produce enough to keep himself alive. There remained only two courses open to him: the threat of a mass walk-out or a rebellion for the strictly limited aim of establishing a reasonable cycle of work.

Sometime in the thirteenth century the serfs of the abbey of Mont-St-Michel arrived at such a situation and they rebelled. Their local revolution was enshrined in a curious poem, *Le conte des vilains de Verson*, by a certain Estout de Goz. His purpose in writing it was to upbraid the villeins for their evil and most unnatural revolt. Throughout his long recital he refers to the villeins with a steady malice, for he shared to the full that active hatred for the peasant which most contemporary poets, themselves pensioners of the villeins' lords, displayed. For them, the villein was a kind of brutal goblin, repulsive in appearance, bestial in morals, his viciousness tempered only by his cowardice. De Goz's open bias makes him an invaluable witness for, after a vague account of the causes of the quarrel, he goes on to list in detail the intolerable burdens that custom had imposed upon the villeins during a yearly cycle. Beginning with the Feast of St John, the villeins mowed the lord's meadow, carried hay to the great barn, cleaned the ditches. In August there was the great grain *corvée*, or forced labour, the securing of the wheat harvests; at the same time they owed sheaves from their own fields as tithe. A month later each supplied the abbey with his best two pigs, and paid a tax on the remainder. In October they paid another tax on their fields and in late autumn they began to sow and harrow winter wheat.

Following that, was a 'gift' of a kind of cake 'for the private room'. De Goz does not explain this purely local method of extracting food, but the later bringing of hens at Christmas was a general imposition. On Palm Sunday came the sheep tithe; at Easter there began the lengthy *corvée* of sowing and harrowing spring wheat; then followed wood cutting and carting. Interspersed with these *corvées* were direct and frequently humiliating taxes. If a man married his daughter outside the seigneury, he paid for the privilege. 'In times past', remarks de Goz, 'the villein took his daughter by the hand and gave her over to his lord.' The three sous' tax he now paid was in redemption of that *jus primae noctis*. If the quality of his various 'gifts' or dues fell below standard the provost of the lord seized the gage which the villein had deposited. As it was the provost who decided whether or not the quality was below standard, fruitful grounds for argument were supplied. The duty the villein owed was disguised under a variety of names but they fell into three groups: forced labour, payment in kind and payment in money. In only one instance does de Goz mention a return payment: they received two deniers a day when they carted wood — a 'rich wage' according to de Goz but small enough when it is considered that the tax on each of the eight pigs a villein was permitted to keep was a denier.

The Growth of Freedom

In the year 987 the abbey of St Arnould granted freedom to the inhabitants of Morvilles-sur-Seille near Metz, the first formal act of manumission of servitude. Over the next century other lords hesitantly followed, their charters of affranchisement containing a mass of qualifications and reservations. The process continued, slowly but gathering momentum until the late twelfth and early thirteenth centuries when there came a spate of charters granting wholesale freedoms over wide areas of the country.

The French principle that the children of a free woman were themselves free meant that, on the whole, men became free at a slightly greater rate than that in which they fell into servitude. Additionally, the manumission of serfs was, in theory, a virtuous act by which a dying man might hope to acquire merit. Nevertheless, no matter how pious a man was, he had a duty towards his heirs. The land he left them was of little value unless there were serfs to work it. The sudden acceleration of manumissions owed little to either natural causes or to piety, but almost everything to considerations of finance, and was a product of that resurgence of national energy which has been called the renaissance of the twelfth century. No one factor in this movement was primary: all were interdependent. The increased power of the central authority; the growth of towns; the revival of trade; the increased use of specie — each contributed to the development of the others and was itself augmented by their increase. And all contributed to lift the peasant from that slough in which he had been engulfed for centuries.

The key to the peasant's freedom was the use of money in place of goods and services. The Crusades had begun the process on a large scale. Almost overnight, hundreds of potential crusading knights found that they had to raise large sums in cash to equip themselves and their retainers. Some sold their lands; the wiser ones commuted their serfs' customary dues to cash payments, either outright or in the form of rents. The development of the towns provided, for the first time in centuries, markets where surplus food could be sold for cash. At the same time the growing luxury trade with the East provided the nobility with an incentive to receive cash instead of goods from their workers. There was little point in offering a travel-stained merchant a flock of sheep for a bolt of silk or measure of spices. The merchant wanted cash which he could transport over thousands of miles in order to obtain more goods. And the lord could only obtain money from the serf if the serf was himself allowed to earn it. An additional source of revenue open to a far-seeing lord was the development of virgin lands, particularly those on the edges of the great forests. A process very similar to the nineteenth-century development of Australia and the Far West of America continued in France until the end of the twelfth century. To develop those areas distant from established centres it was necessary to found settlements and to attract workers to them by the promise of a better life. That promise was contained in charters which clearly detailed the rights and duties of both serf and lord. The lord wanted revenue, not produce, and the principle was therefore established at the very beginning of a new settlement that the serfs were free to sell their produce and the lord obtained his revenue in the form of rents.

The monarch approved the franchises granted by territorial lords for they acted as a dissolvent of the feudal microcosms. Nevertheless, he jealously conserved the right of ownership of royal serfs, granting them their freedom for the identical reasons of finance as did all other lords. In 1315 Louis X made a proclamation which, taken at its face value, could have been the manifesto of a revolution. 'Since, according to the rights of nature, each man is born free… and considering that our kingdom is named and called the Kingdom of the Franks, and wishing that the thing should be in verity according to the name we have ordered and ordained that throughout our kingdom servitudes shall cease.' The true motive of the noble declaration appeared a few days later when a rider was added, stating that 'because of bad counsel some serfs prefer to remain in the wretchedness of servitude rather than enter into the state of franchise', and they would therefore be taxed as much as they could bear. Louis had hoped to gain more in taxes from free men than in work from serfs; the suspicious serfs, preferring to remain in a known condition rather than pay heavily for an uncertain one, had to be coerced.

The cautious reservations made in charters of affranchisement were well illustrated by the famous wholesale manumissions effected by the cathedral of Notre-Dame in Paris in the latter half of the thirteenth century. The *Grand Pastoral* recorded manumissions granted not merely to individuals but to entire villages, among them Vitry-sur-Seine, Bagneux, Châtenay and Orly. All the charters were similar to that of Orly where the inhabitants, 'having admitted that they were the people of the abbey of Notre-Dame, of servile condition, subject to the canons of the church from time immemorial... and on their supplications and oft-repeated prayers and in considerations of piety... and on the conditions enumerated...', were to receive their freedom. It was a strictly relative term, the innumerable qualifications effectively cancelling out the claim to piety. The serfs were no longer to be taxed *a merci* but were to pay an annual tax of 60 francs — apart from the same tax which the king levied. They were to continue the payment of tithes, were to submit to the *corvées*, particularly the repairing of roads and, above all, promised to call in no other authority but the chapter to settle their differences. On these conditions, and for the price of 4,000 livres to be paid in eight years — during which time *mainmorte* was still to be exacted — the chapter granted them manumission.

The chapter gained immediately far more than it had lost. Apart from the considerable outright payment and the continuance of tithes and the regular tax, it still had the right to the large reserve of free labour represented by the *corvées*. The late serfs had gained an intangible, immeasurable thing — personal freedom, with its rights to buy and sell, to marry where they chose, to leave the land. It was a tiny seed but it was to grow.

2: URBAN SOCIETY

The Commune and the Town

The gradual freeing of the rural serf was an erosion of the very base of feudalism. The opposite reaction — the grouping of men into urban communities — came as a wedge which was to shatter the rest of the fabric. The development of that wedge was rapid. The first communes did not come into existence until late in the eleventh century; barely three generations later, a hitherto unknown class, the *bourgeois* were so firmly established that their members could be included in a royal council of regency. The speed of the change was reflected by the poets, ever the most alert to changing conditions. Before the twelfth century the action of the *chansons* took place almost exclusively in rural surroundings, moving between the castle of the noble, the battlefield and the meadows of May. Now the praise of cities was sung, their beauties and wealth described as though they were persons. The chroniclers, too, turned aside from their endless cataloguing of the deeds of the great to describe, with enthusiasm, the urban homes of the commonalty. 'Ghent, proud of its houses ornamented with towers. Ypres, famous for its wool-dyeing. Caen, so full of churches, houses and inhabitants that she found herself scarcely inferior to Paris. Tours, proud of its citizens. Nantes, enriched by the fish-filled Loire.' So rims William of Armorica's eulogy and its almost Italianate pride in urbanity finds echoes in other chroniclers, both monkish and lay.

An urban community was linked to a lord in precisely the same manner as a rural community. The nucleus of many towns was the castle of the lord and, for long, *château* and *ville* were synonymous terms. Plurality of lords was the norm, the *bourg*, or suburb, usually being governed as an entity distinct from the town proper. But whether there were one lord or many, each demanded his dues from the inhabitants exactly as the rural lord demanded his dues from the peasant. Here, however, the fields that were to be ploughed were industrial and the harvest that was reaped was money. The increase in the size and prosperity of the towns emphasised the anachronism of feudal dues: the yield of a tax could increase ten or one hundred times as the industry developed, while the contribution of the lord sank to nil. Secure behind great walls, the inhabitants had less and less need of a man whose only trade was war, together with his expensive train.

The movement which resulted in the communes in the eleventh century was less a revolt against feudalism than a modification of it. A commune was itself a feudal personality no less than an individual lord, for it transferred to itself, unchanged, all the rights and ceremonies that once were attached to one man. The transfer was attended with less or more violence depending upon the degree of power exercised by the lord. In general, the communes were established by violence in the north and by negotiation in the south. The great maritime cities of the Mediterranean coast had long held almost independent existence: thus Marseilles had its own navy and both Narbonne and Montpellier could ally themselves with Genoa. The cities of Provence, that daughter of Italy, maintained in their corporate lives much of the independence of those Italian communes which were actual city-states. Arles, Avignon and Marseilles even proclaimed themselves republics at one stage and, though they were rapidly suppressed, in the easier climate of the south they continued to enjoy many rights unknown to the cities of the north. Beyond the Loire, the movement erupted into violence because its pretensions were met with violence. Guibert, Abbot of Nogent, an honourable priest and a temperate writer, spoke with the authentic voice of the feudal lord when he described the word *commune* as 'a new and execrable name. This is what it means — serfs, against law and justice, withdraw themselves from the power of their lords. They pay now only once a year to their lords what they owe them. If they commit some crime they have merely to submit to a fine legally fixed.' Later, the wiser of these lords saw that there was more profit to be obtained from the free man than the serf and even initiated negotiations. But, in the early stages, they saw only the destruction of the existing order of things and the total loss of their means of subsistence.

Among the first of the towns to establish a commune was Le Mans, the citizens taking advantage of the absence of their great duke in 1066. They timorously gave up the keys when William returned in power but others were braver — or more fortunate in having irresolute lords. Cambrai followed in 1076, then St Quentin, Beauvais, Arras, Noyon, Laon, Amiens. Noyon was unusually fortunate in its bishop who, both wisely and humanely, anticipated events and not only 'prevailed upon our lord King Louis to grant this commune and corroborate it with the King's seal', but threatened with excommunication those who would presume to violate it. Elsewhere, the ecclesiastic lords were the most bitter opponents of the new movement.

Guibert gave a vivid first-hand account of the violence that attended the birth of the commune of Laon. His abbey was not far from the town and he was personally acquainted with its bishop, Gaudry, a peculiarly brutal example of the fighting priest. Although there was no doubting his view on the morality of the commune, throughout his recital Guibert shows himself appalled at the cynicism displayed by both the clerics and nobility of Laon.

Gaudry had taken himself off to England and, during his absence, the people freed themselves — peacefully, via the agency of the lay and ecclesiastic lords. In Guibert's words, 'the clergy, the archdeacon and the knights, seeing how things were going, and for the sake of gaining money, made an offer to the people to give them, for a financial consideration, the power of forming a commune. The men of the people grasped this opportunity to free themselves from a host of vexations, gave large sums of money to these misers, whose hands seemed like gulfs which must be filled. They promised the people, under oath, to keep to the letter the agreements made with them.' Gaudry returned, stormed, then was himself placated by a substantial payment. There was one more payment to be made and this the people paid to the King, Louis the Fat, in the following year.

Until this point, clergy, nobility and monarch seemed to have looked upon the payments they received merely as a novel, but welcome, method of extracting additional revenue. A year later Gaudry changed his mind and persuaded Louis easily enough to withdraw the charter. The entire town then went on strike and Gaudry, with a cynical and dangerous indifference to the earlier transactions and to earlier oaths sworn on relics, demanded another payment equal to all that which had already been paid out. It was a foolish move of a man who was ever more knave than fool. Doubtless he felt that an oath to a serf was as binding as an oath to an animal and that Laon, with all that was in it, was his by divine and natural right. But the people had tasted freedom and tasted the value of peaceful negotiations. They rose in tumult, murdered Gaudry, enlisted the support of a local baron, rebelled even against the king.

They were defeated and their city sacked, yet so strong was this flood towards the commune that, in 1128, just four years afterwards, they received their charter anew and this time retained it.

The charter of the commune of Beauvais was a typical expression of the spirit of association, for it emphasised the proposition that the inhabitants of a city formed a single body. 'All the men residing within the walls of the city — to whatever lord they may belong [or] the land which they occupy — shall swear the commune. The peers of the commune shall swear to favour no one for friendship's sake, injure no one on the grounds of private enmity.' Communal privilege was balanced by communal liability. 'Whenever any man has done injury to a person who has sworn the commune... the peers of the commune shall punish the delinquent. If anyone does injury to a person who comes to Beauvais for trading purposes the peers shall punish the malefactor — unless the merchant be an enemy of the commune.' In the delicate matter of relationship with local lords the charter was prudent but firm. 'If a culprit takes refuge in some castle, the peers of the commune shall refer to the lord of the castle and, if, according to their opinion, satisfaction is done against the enemy of the commune, it will be enough. But, if the lord refuses satisfaction, they shall do justice on the lord's property or on his retainers.' The Beauvoisis must have felt very confident in themselves to enunciate, categorically, their intention to revenge themselves on any baron who denied them justice. It was a remarkable demonstration of independence by a hitherto unknown body of men. Even a century later, William of Armorica could record his delight and amazement at the fact that the people of Mantes dared defy Henry II of England as though they were his equals. He placed in Henry's mouth sentiments which must have been echoed scores of times by French nobles.

> What is this French foolishness and whence comes this presumption? The common people of Mantes, which numbers scarcely 5,000 souls, dare to think of measuring themselves against the innumerable army of my knights. Those folk who ought rather to burrow into their caves and barricade themselves behind their gates, march upon our naked swords.

The spirit of the commune was little more democratic than the spirit of a feudal tenure. The impetus for its establishment came from the middle ranges of society, emanating from those men who sought their livelihood neither in producing goods nor in warfare but in trade. They included indeed those members of the nobility who deemed themselves no less noble because they lived on the produce of artisans instead of the produce of peasants. And just as the artisans were later to form themselves into corporations, so these patricians formed themselves into mutual protection societies called fraternities. Their charters stressed the need of unity making of it a virtue: 'through the love of neighbour we aspire to the love of God'. The ordinances ranged over every aspect of social man from the prescription of a drinking bout to the provision of insurance. Each member was to be prepared to contribute to the ransom of a brother or his merchandise should they fall into the hands of a brigand. Members of the fraternity travelled together and a brother who left his arms behind was fined for weakening the common defence. Similarly, if two merchants were together in a strange town, the one who finished his business first was to wait for the other so that they could leave the town together. If one brother struck another, he would be expelled from the society. The Fraternity of Valenciennes met regularly in a curious ceremony that was part religious, part convivial. Prayers opened the meeting and even during the drinking session singing was forbidden and each brother could speak only to the man next to him.

The fraternities were exclusive: some even had a clause in their charter which explicitly forbade a brother to go to the assistance of a member of another fraternity. When a commune was established, its officers were drawn entirely from this wealthy section of the community, workers being excluded from the magistracy either explicitly or by the inevitable process of nepotism. Beaumanoir remarked upon it: 'So it happens that some are dean, or mayor, or sworn members and the next year they create [officers] from their brothers, their nephews, or their near relatives so that in ten or twelve years all the rich people have their part in the administration of the good towns.' The artisans with whom they had allied themselves in the original struggle for power were first dispossessed, then actively exploited. Jacques de Vitry adds the wealthy burgher to his dismal catalogue of despoilers of the poor: 'the burgesses, relying on their numbers, oppress their neighbours and subject them by violence.' Internecine struggle took the place of concerted revolt against the territorial lord. The cities of the south even found it necessary to introduce the Italian system of the *podestà*, the appointment of a foreigner who would be above all factional interests, as supreme official in a commune. And, should they succeed in making even transient peace within their own walls, they began war outside. 'They aim at the ruin of their neighbours: the majority of the communes make rapid war upon each other.'

Fierce factional struggles between wealthy families and between workers and patricians within the communes, and commercial warfare between commune and commune: this was the new pattern that superseded the old over large areas. The progress of France towards a multiplicity of tiny city-states on the Italian model would have gone far had it not been for the presence of a monarchy with ever-growing power. In the first days of the commune the attitude of the monarch had been ambiguous. Louis the Fat, the so-called 'Father of the Communes', had played a sinister part in the suppression of Laon. The monarch in general aided the commune when its establishment eroded the power of the baron; he became its enemy when it encroached upon the power of his ally, the Church, or upon his own. In all the royal domains only Dreux and Senlis succeeded in obtaining a commune; Orleans attempted one and was crushed, Paris never knew one. But in the final stage of the commune it was the monarch who interfered, crushing the power of the dominant families and introducing his own rule of law. These exclusive groups of wealthy merchants, nominally communes, were a dead end in the development of the towns. The future lay with those towns directly controlled by the king, who granted a charter of liberties but continued to govern, and the new towns established by territorial lords.

A new town was established for the same reason that new villages were founded — in order to increase the revenue of a lord. In them, town planning found a place for the first time since the days of Rome. Four crosses were placed at the cardinal points and, within the limits traced out, the plan of the new town came into existence: church, town hall, market place, squares, streets. Sometimes the name given to the new community was taken from some famous existing town as

Florence (Fleurance), Cordoba (Cordes), Pampeluna (Pampelonne). More commonly they were a description of the status of the new community and took such names as Villeneuve, Neuville, Neufchâteau, Villefranche. Sauvetat, Sauveterre also appeared, derived from *sauveté* — a refuge — for in their charters they explicitly granted the right of sanctuary to any man who would take up residence as a citizen.

By the time of Philip Augustus the *bourgeois* had emerged as a recognisable class. The most dramatic recognition of their status came in 1190 when Philip Augustus established a council of regency before leaving for the Crusade. The great ones of the nation naturally found themselves on the council — the relatives of the king, the great feudal lords. But in addition to these he appointed another council to act as watchdog over the other — and on this council were six burghers of Paris. For the first time the names of humble men appear along with the resounding titles of the nobility in an instrument of government: Ébrouin the Moneychanger, Othon of the Grève, Robert of Chartres, Thiboud the Rich, Baldwin Bruneau, Nicolas Boisseau. They were charged with the control of the treasury, were issued with the Great Seal of the realm. The diplomas they issued contained the formula 'under the witness of our *bourgeois*'. The king had no intention of permanently sharing his powers with this humble stratum of his kingdom and revoked them on his return. But it was a foretaste of future power. The Third Estate had come into existence, shouldering aside that ancient division of society which classified men simply as those who worked, those who prayed, those who fought.

The Corps de Métiers

Some time about the year 1090 a humble painter by the name

of Fulcon arrived at the monastery of St-Aubin, Angers, seeking work. He seems to have impressed the abbot with his ability for he was offered the long-term job of making all the windows in the monastery, as well as the execution of such paintings as he was instructed to do from time to time. Fulcon, however, was not a serf of the monastery and before he could start work it was necessary to regularise the position. He was to be treated as a brother and, as payment for his work, he was to be given a fief, consisting of a vineyard and house, which was to revert to the monastery at his death. Thus neatly fitted into the social hierarchy, Fulcon began work and passed out of history.

At much the same time in Chartres, Léobin, a carpenter of that city, contracted to do the odd jobs about the bishop's palace. He already had his own little shop but agreed to go to the palace as required and, in return for his work, he was to receive a specified amount and type of food: bread, wine, an occasional chicken or piece of meat and the right to eat with the domestic servants. The work he was to perform and its returns were alike humble but the lengthy contract which specified his duties had a resounding title, 'This is the fief of Léobin the carpenter'.

The fiefs of these two humble men were the product of a twilight period. Neither quite independent workmen nor yet seigneurial chattels, their working life was regulated under the old forms while they themselves practised a new.

There were thousands of men like them in the towns. Originally they would have been the artisans of a great household and, just as their rural fellows gained the freedom to sell some of their agricultural produce, so these urban serfs began, little by little, to sell the products of their workshop. And, little by little, they learned the virtue of co-operation among themselves. The formation of the *corps de métiers*, the artisans' associations, developed independently of the communal movement, beginning as associations of men not necessarily of the same trade, but of the same status. Only later did each begin to specialise and, with that specialisation came exclusiveness and, finally, a tyranny as complete in its little world as that ever exercised by the associations of rich merchants.

The most ancient of the *corps de métiers* were those of the butchers and bakers. Trades so vital to the public health came under the control of a civic authority from the earliest days, and by the time the first associations of other workers were being formed, these two constituted a species of aristocracy. A charter of 1134 speaks of the already ancient establishment of the butchers, which was then powerful enough to enforce that principle of nepotism which was ultimately to destroy the entire system: no one but the son of a butcher could hope to become a master. The bakers of Paris vigorously defended themselves against an attempt to enforce the seigneurial monopoly of the ban oven. Ordinary members of the public had to submit to the destruction of their ovens or pay a heavy tax in lieu, but the bakers were able to cite a royal ordinance that had long since freed them from the monopoly. The wealth and power of these two trade associations provided the best possible argument for co-operations and those workers newly free of their lord swiftly followed the example.

In 1261 St Louis appointed Étienne Boileau to the office of Provost of Paris. The powers of the office were wide, for the Provost controlled military service, police, finance and justice within the limits of Paris, acting as the king's major-domo. It was therefore singularly vulnerable to corruption and corruption duly appeared, the office being sold to the highest bidder who then recouped his heavy expenses, and made a profit, by open bribery. But the office was also a vital instrument of government and St Louis, in appointing Boileau, intended a reformation. He could not have chosen a better man. Boileau set about his task of cleansing and reconstruction with energy and, during it, turned his attention to the activities of the *corps de métiers* for whose control he was now responsible. The daily life of Paris depended upon them and that life was slowly being throttled by the abuses inherent in a monopoly: bad workmanship, high prices, deception of a gullible populace, all these were practised in greater or less degree by each corporation. They were, however, powerful and Boileau went about his work discreetly. Each corporation was invited to submit its statutes to him, revised if necessary, and he published them all in one compilation, the *Book of Trades*, whose preamble delicately hinted at the reason for its existence. 'Because some things were not as good and honest as they could have been', the regulations of the corporations were here presented for the guidance of the craftsmen — and of the public. The *Book of Trades* listed some corporations in Paris with a total of 5,000 masters. Fifty years later the number had doubled, partly as a result of the development in new trades but mainly because of increasing specialisation within trades. There were measurers of wheat, wood, salt; porters of water, plaster, wheat, salt and wood; sellers of fresh-water and salt-water fish.

The names of the corporations varied not merely from place to place but from trade to trade. Here they were *corps de métiers*, the most general term; there they were guilds, *commun de métier*, *charité*, *confrérie*, these last two names being indicative of that spirit which originally moved them. Equally varied were the names of the offices of the corporations: *prud'hommes*, *jureurs*, *bailis*, syndics. These men formed a council with an elected president known, in the north, as the mayor, and were responsible for the general administration of the corporation — including the fining of recalcitrant members, the maintenance of a minimum standard of workmanship, the organisation of festivals and social insurance. Above them, in Paris, was the Provost who was directly responsible for those aspects of a craft that touched the public good or safety. Thus beer was only allowed to be brewed if the harvest were abundant enough to provide a surplus for the purpose.

Masters in 40 of the trades listed in Boileau's Statute were permitted to take as many apprentices as they wished. These trades were for the most part linked with the production of food and included the coopers, millers, grain dealers, brewers, and sellers of salt. The masters in all other trades were limited to three apprentices at the most, each master being permitted to take on a new apprentice when the old was within a year of finishing his time. The apprentice paid a premium varying between 20 and 100 sous: the period of the apprenticeship varied greatly, running from four years for the rope-makers through eight years for the shieldmakers to the maximum, 12 years, for the *paternôtriers* or rosary-makers. Theoretically, the length of the apprenticeship was supposed to ensure that the future craftsman would learn every possible aspect of his craft: in practice, it was used to keep down the numbers of potential competitors. There was no clear-cut relationship between length of service and type of work. Obviously, the apprentice jeweller would need a far longer period in which to perfect his demanding craft than would an apprentice rope-maker, if for no better reason than that his mistakes were more costly to his master. But within a craft the amount of premium paid and length of service demanded were largely fixed arbitrarily. There were three different corporations of *paternôtriers*: the masters of one demanded a premium of 20 sous and ten years' apprenticeship, while the others demanded 46 sous and six years and 46 sous and ten years respectively. The length of apprenticeship could therefore be reduced in exchange for an increased premium.

The engagement of the apprentice was made in the form of a contract, drawn up by a notary, witnessed usually by two masters of the corporation and then deposited in the archives. The traditional picture of the apprentice as a rollicking, irresponsible youth learning his trade under the benign eye of an elder is hardly borne out by the testimony of the records of the corporations. The apprentice became the absolute property of the master, even as the serf had been the absolute property of the lord. He could be sold to any other master: if he escaped he was sought and brought back by force if need. The expense of the search was borne by the master who was thereby hardly rendered better disposed to his wayward apprentice. After three such escapades the master relinquished all responsibility towards the lad who would never again find employment within that craft. Accounts of brutality towards an apprentice are recorded as a matter of course in the archives. One master struck his apprentice in the face with a bunch of keys, making a great hole in his cheek, when the boy's father attempted to revoke the articles of apprenticeship. Girls were not immune. Isabelle Béraude, apprenticed to Jean Bruières, died as a result of her master's brutality. On this occasion the Bailli of St Germain-des-Prés was officially notified and Bruières probably paid the penalty.

The apprentice who had finished his time became a *valet*, free to work for whom he pleased for a standard rate of pay. Under pain of fine, each had to go every morning to a specific public place where the *valets* of his craft gathered for hiring. Their working day lasted some 16 hours in summer and eight in winter. Night work, when allowed by the statutes, was compulsory but was obviously unpopular, for time and again the annals record that some particular worker was penalised for refusing to work at night. Those trades which demanded some delicacy of touch — jewellers, certain types of weavers, candle-makers, buckle-makers, cutlers — were not allowed to work after sunset 'because the clarity of the light is not sufficient for said work'. The causes of strikes were invariably related to the length of hours or some attempt on the part of the masters to reduce the rate of pay. The annals of the crafts go into few details for they were written on behalf of the masters, but the casual references that creep in show that grievances sometimes boiled over into insurrection. The natural tendency of the workers to form trade unions within their craft was firmly suppressed. In Beauvais the ordinance was promulgated that: 'Alliances in which any sort of people agree or pledge themselves not to work for so low a rate as before and thus cause their wage to be increased and threaten their comrades who refuse to join, are against the common good.' In 1258 the Bailli of Rouen forbade the weavers ever again to meet in their customary place, because of their 'conspirations, murmurings and desire to increase the price of their work and other such villainies to the damage of the commune of the drapers and the town of Rouen'. This bald statement conceals what must have been an interesting situation: the weavers had presumably got together while awaiting hiring and decided to force up their wages. In Flanders, the workers resorted to violence. The weavers of Douai, smarting beneath a new and unjust tax, rioted and murdered 11 sheriffs, and the Count of Flanders had to take military action against them. In Ypres the masters attempted to conceal a wage cut by adding an hour to the day: their workers rebelled and murdered the mayor. The masters in many cities, however, recognised the danger which one bad master could bring to all. In Montpellier they made themselves collectively responsible for any master who attempted to cheat his workmen. If convicted of such an attempt, he was denied labour for a specific period and forced to make a large donation to charity.

The coveted title of master was not automatically given even to a man who had finished his time. Heavy payments were necessary: to the lord of the city in recognition of his feudal right; to the corporation; to each brother master. In Paris, 30 of the corporations belonged to the lord — who here was the King — and the would-be master had to purchase the right to work from him. Elsewhere, certain nobles had bought this right and retailed it in their turn. At the time that Étienne Boileau was drawing up his Statute the King made over to Foulques du Temple the right over 'all manner of workers with the blade — that is to say coopers, boat-and ship-builders, turners and all manner of work relating to carpentry'. Foulques received a tax from each master, appointed a *prud'homme* in each of the crafts, and sat in judgement over them.

The new master's entry into his craft was solemn. The mayor read aloud the statutes of the corporation and the candidate swore on the relics of saints faithfully to observe the rules and loyally to assist his brothers. The millers of the Grand-Pont in Paris, liable to be exposed to the dangers brought about by a sudden flood, promised to go to their neighbour's aid if required by day or by night. The master then acted as host to his brothers at a reception in which all drank freely, following which he was inscribed in the registers. Even after this there was a probation period varying from a year and a day for the cobblers to three years for the bakers. But after probation he could never be deprived of his rights, save for the most grave faults, and transmitted them to his wife. Widows of a master were deemed to be free of a craft and could practise exactly as their husbands had done.

A high proportion of the regulations of corporations were aimed at the prevention of fraud. Goldsmiths were to use only gold of the Paris assay 'which is the best in the world'; chandlers were to use only one piece of wax in the making of a candle. Cutlers were forbidden to put silver ornaments on to handles of bone — which could too easily be passed off as ivory: white wood was not to be covered with either brass, lead or iron. The master was held responsible for the work done by his men. Thus the drapers forbade their masters to occupy two workshops if it meant crossing the street to get from one to the other. The public itself was engaged as a watchdog by the general ordinance that all crafts were to be carried out, in daylight, in full public view. Goldsmiths and locksmiths were obliged to have their forges in their shops: the work-benches of tailors and bucklers were to be placed near the window, less in the interest of their eyesight than to allow the constant casual inspection of passers-by. Officers of the corporation made frequent visits — unannounced, to ensure that standards were being maintained. Bad food or merchandise was seized and burnt, not infrequently with the accompaniment of violence. The annals of the bakers of Ypres contain a bald account of what must have been a first-class row. The wife of Warmer, a baker of the town, hid bread which had been declared to be bad and refused entry to the shop by the *prud'hommes* when they came to confiscate it. They forced their way in and carried it off but she followed them down the road, displaying some of the loaves in a basket, shrieking to the people to come and see if the bread was not good. She and her husband were fined on three accounts: for having made bad bread, for refusing entry to the officers and for attempting to excite a public tumult. It would have been interesting to have Warmer's comments on his wife's loyalty.

3: THE CONTEMPORARY WORLD

The Sources of Knowledge

Two main elements could be distinguished in man's view of Creation. The one was the result of a rigorous intellectual discipline which, stretching words to the very limit of meaning, sought to define the eternally indefinable. This discipline could degenerate into a mere play of words, of the kind which astonished John of Salisbury when he returned to Paris to find that all the world seemed to have gone mad on dialectics. It was directly responsible for the torture and death of thousands of Christians for, in defining truth, it must necessarily define untruth, and, in defending orthodoxy, it created heresy. But it stemmed from a desire to establish a grammar of meaning which would be eternally constant. Its premises and objects now are questionable, but the tools it devised to link them became part of the intellectual heritage of the world.

Co-existing with this worship of logic, this ice-cold evaluation of the spiritual universe, was a habit of thought which instinctively preferred the impossible to the probable, the marvellous to the mundane, and presented its conclusions in concrete images. That love of symbolism which permeated every stratum of society was a manifestation of the dual process. A symbol was at once an abstraction of the idea and the thing itself, so that a vassal receiving a sod of turf from his lord was receiving not merely a token but that actual portion of the planet which was now his fief. The supreme example of this ability to receive as one entity two apparently conflicting ideas was the almost universal faith in the miracle of transubstantiation, the consecrated bread that changed but did not change. With this belief as a keystone, the acceptance of the miraculous as an element of daily life was a commonplace.

In 1245 a certain friar of Metz in Lorraine, called Gossuin, conceived the idea of making a species of encyclopedia. It was not the first of its kind, nor the last, but Gossuin's ability to give outrageous fiction the same weight as that accorded to demonstrable fact touched some public chord and the work became immensely popular. His *Image du Monde* is cast in the form of a poem and its metrical construction was the extent of his original contribution: the contents were the work of other men, for Gossuin shared to the full the prevailing indifference to anything resembling copyright. A written thought was no more the property of the writer than a spoken thought was the property of the speaker, and Gossuin therefore harvested where he wished. The names of the great were mentioned with pride — Gossuin spoke of Ptolemy as though he were superhuman — while smaller men were fortunate to receive a passing mention by name. Jacques de Vitry's *Historia hierosolymitana*, Honorius's *Imago mundi*, Einhard's *Life of Charlemagne*, all these and more were ransacked to provide a lengthy poem written in the dialect of Lorraine. Gossuin saw his task as that of a synthesist, bringing together into a manageable whole the work of men scattered over the centuries and over the known world. He did his work so well as to imperil his own chance of literary immortality, for others took his work sometimes in parts, sometimes as a whole, and, in their turn, made it their own. A few years after he had finished another man of Lorraine re-wrote the whole thing. This second writer had a love of stories and introduced them at every opportunity, sometimes with grotesque effect. But he also added eye-witness accounts of some of the marvels of which Gossuin knew only by report — particularly the wonderful smoking mountain of Sicily: 'I, who made this book, have seen this second mountain', and he goes on to describe how he climbed it so that he was even above the sound of thunder, how he held his hands to the heat and, most marvellous of all, how he was able to quench his thirst with snow in this outpost of hell.

Two hundred years after Gossuin and his continuator had completed their work, William Caxton found a prose translation of it and turned it into English under the title of *The Mirrour of the World*. It had become something of a museum piece by then and here and there Caxton corrected or argued with its author. As far as Gossuin was concerned, Europe ended at the Mons Jovis — the Great St Bernard: Greece, Italy, Spain, Portugal, Aragon, Lombardy are all classified as Africa. Caxton, as a good translator, dutifully follows but could not resist adding 'howbeit that the Auctor of this book saye that thise contress ben in Affryke yet, as I understonde, alle thise ben within the lymytes and boundes of Europe'. But Caxton was heir to the increased knowledge of the past 200 years. His own translation, though of a high standard, throws some light on the origins of marvels. Gossuin, speaking of the Balearic Islands, described its inhabitants as being skilful in the use of the sling (*la fondè*). Caxton mistook the noun for foundry (*fonte*) and thereby endowed the islanders with skill in melting metals. Gossuin himself was victim of a similar error. One of his original authors spoke of a tribe in India who lived upon sea-fish — '*ex mari viventes*'. At some stage '*viventes*' became changed to '*bibentes*', creating a remarkable race of people who drank nothing but sea-water. Many a miracle was due to the humdrum fact of a scribe's ignorance or laziness in copying.

Garbled traditions emanating from the writers of the Classic world, strengthened by some solid knowledge of astronomy, ornamented with fables, coloured with a little personal knowledge and the whole strung together on a moralising theme — this was the image of the world. Gossuin was aware that some of his miracles might choke the most gullible — but let such a man beware. Is the Creator not capable of an infinite number of marvels? And in any case, Gossuin adds with sound common sense, the miraculous is only relative. The race of giants marvel at us for our small size even as the race of pigmies marvel at us for our giant stature. And if the centicore has the foot of a horse, it is also true to say that the horse has the foot of a centicore.

Gossuin paid great homage to those noble Ancients from whom, after God, all knowledge came and did not fail to use their integrity as a stick to beat the degenerate scholars of his own day. The Ancients lived for knowledge for its own sake; the scholars of the University of Paris today study merely to prepare themselves for rich professions like so many courtiers or merchants. The Ancients gave away their possessions and lived frugally — which incidentally explains why people lived as much as 30 years longer than they do today. The rich clerks of today consider only the acquisition of money and its symbols: they acquire valuable books but lavish all their pride and love upon the sumptuous bindings, not the sacred contents. Who, then, were these giants of Antiquity and how did their knowledge survive the cataclysms of history? In Gossuin's hand time becomes telescoped: Adam and Noah, Julius Caesar and Plato, Boethius and Ptolemy share a similar world. His great guide was Ptolemy, appearing as the famous King Tolomeus of Egypt, 'one of the many kings of that name'. He it was who invented the clock and the calendar which Julius Caesar of Rome revised and which is now used in the ordering of the Church's year. It is not clear whether

Gossuin thought this King Tolomeus lived before or after the Flood, but certainly he knew more of the master science of astronomy than any mortal man, save only Adam. After the Fall, the race of Adam addressed themselves to the study of the skies; over 2,000 years passed before they were again able to codify the Seven Arts which Adam had known and lost. In their work these Ancients had perceived certain signs which told them the Earth would be destroyed by fire or by flood and, so that knowledge should not perish, they built two mighty pillars, the one of brick to resist fire and the other of marble to resist flood, and engraved the Seven Arts upon them. Shem discovered the marble pillar after the Flood and re-established the science of astronomy which Abraham developed. Plato came, followed by his clerk Aristotle, and these two divined the mystery of the Trinity. But they were Saracens, knowing no Latin, so they wrote in Greek: Boethius translated their books into the universal language. There were other men who wandered through the world seeking marvels and wisdom: Apollonius, who passed the flood of Ganges and all Ind and discovered the Golden Table of the Sun and came at last to the end of the world where there were no more ways; Alexander, who went to the bottom of the sea in a glass barrel to study monsters of the deep. And there was Virgil, the necromancer.

The transformation of Virgil the poet into Virgil the dark magician is one of the odder metempsychoses that Gossuin records. He was following a very old tradition, based on Virgil's supposed gift of prophecy as shown in his foretelling of Christ's birth in the Fourth Eclogue. By Gossuin's day the purely theological appeal of the prophecy had become confused and enriched by a tradition which saw Virgil as another Merlin. He was a little, hunchbacked man who walked always with his head bent to the ground, and who owed all his wisdom to astronomy. He made a brazen fly that kept all other flies away and a brazen horse whose gaze would cure a sick horse. He built a great city upon an egg in such a way that, when the egg was touched, the city moved. He built a hanging garden high above the Earth, constructed a bridge so subtly that no one could see how it was suspended; revenged himself upon an Emperor's daughter by extinguishing all the fires in Rome so that everyone had to go to her for light. Yet he was in the end betrayed by his own skill, for he made a brazen head which foretold the future and, seeking his usual daily guidance of it, he was misled and went out into the sun and suffered mortal sunstroke. He was buried in Sicily, not far from the sea but some of his marvels — the brazen fly and horse and the egg — are to be seen to this day in Naples.

And, having presented his credentials, Gossuin raises the curtain on the contemporary picture of the world — that round sphere moving to the accompaniment of celestial music: tiny compared with its sisters but bearing upon it the works of the Creator. The writers of later centuries would be forced to go to these other planets for the marvels ever desired of man. Gossuin was more fortunate: marvels began on the other side of the hill.

The Image of the World

The world is round like a ball, and the sky encloses it like a shell encloses the egg. The sky is filled with a spiritual air — the ether — which offers no resistance to light. The angels cross this to bring their messages to Earth but mortal creatures would perish in it, just as the fish perishes in air.

The four elements that compose the world — fire, air, water and earth — are disposed concentrically even as, in the egg, one finds white under the shell, then yellow, then a spot of grease. Earth is the heaviest and is therefore at the centre and, because it is round, if one man were to walk east and another west, they would meet at the Antipodes. If a hole were bored through the Earth, the sky would be visible on the other side. Gossuin here explains that it is possible to so carve a globe that a plan can be made. On this plan a line would be visible which divided north from south: this is the Equator and upon it is the strange city called Aaron where astronomy was discovered.

Only one quarter of the globe is inhabitable and this quarter is itself divided into three regions: Asia, as big as the other two put together, Europe and Africa. The most important part of Asia is Paradise with its Tree of Life still guarded by flames and the fountain whence rises Ganges, Nile, Tigris and Euphrates. But though the Garden of Eden is still upon the physical Earth no man may ever visit it, for the deserts that surround it are patrolled by most evil and ferocious wild animals. The true terrestrial Paradise is India and particularly that island of Taprobane (Ceylon) which each year has two winters and two summers and a climate so temperate that a man may rejoice in Paradise while yet in the flesh. Pseudo-memories of the Golden Age combine with garbled travellers' tales to furnish India with marvels sufficient to fill a universe. Here trees bear wool as only animals do in other, less fortunate regions, and the vines are so rich that one man can scarcely carry a single bunch. Gold and precious stones abound, but the rich mines are guarded by dragons and griffins each capable of carrying off an armoured knight and his horse. Gossuin's India is largely a mythical place, the receptacle for all marvels that cannot be placed nearer home for fear of immediate contradiction. But it is also the sub-continent of reality and some of its features are derived from observation. The myriad religious customs of the land probably account for many of the more curious races of humans, including those people 'strange but courteous' who live entirely upon the smell of a certain apple, or those others who eat their relatives to do them honour. Some of the animals are recognisable, although their characteristics are bizarre. The elephant seizes its prey with an external bowel attached to its head and the Indians devised traps of brass inhuman shape and filled them with hot cinders to deter the animal from man-eating. The tiger has a blue or multi-coloured body: its prey could escape if they cast mirrors behind because the tiger would presume that its reflection was a cub and would linger to comfort it. The beaver, hunted for its testicles, would sever them in order to escape — a habit observed in Europe. But other monsters could come only from the pages of a mythology. The centicore with horns of a stag, chest of a lion, feet of a horse and voice of a human; another, amphibious monster compounded of horse, elephant and boar with movable horns; the unicorn and the phoenix — viewed from distant France, however, these would appear neither more nor less improbable than the elephant and so were duly recorded.

Sources for the description of the eastern Mediterranean were the Bible and the classics, eked out by the stories of pilgrims and Crusaders. Each country is dismissed with a single distinguishing characteristic; Chaldea, home of the Magi; Persia, birthplace of necromancy; Delos, the first land to appear after the Flood; Scylla, the isle of the Cyclops and, near it, a great island as large as Europe and Africa combined. This was Atlantis, sunk beneath the sea for its sins. Nearer at home, and there is some attempt at verisimilitude but marvels still out-number the mundane. The English have tails — it is the author of the second version of the *Image* who slips in this hoary insult. In Ireland there is a burning region called Purgatory: here a non-repentant sinner will disappear completely and others will suffer according to the degree of their sin. In certain regions of France people measure the beauty of women by the size of the enormous goitres that hang from their throats.

Beneath the Earth is Hell, a locality as real as India. It is an evil and a dreadful place but Gossuin resists the temptation to describe its horrors. It is possible to acquire some idea of Hell upon this Earth, for there are certain burning islands and smoking mountains that are entrances to the abode of the damned.

Leaving Earth, Gossuin passes on to consider Air. He explains with some precision the cycle of moisture and then discourses on electric storms. Lightning is caused by the force of winds in collision: thunder is the sound heard when the red-hot thunderbolts are abruptly extinguished by the moisture in clouds.

The diameter of the Earth is 20428 milles and each mille is composed of 1,000 paces of 5 feet. The circumference is 70,000 miles. The Moon is 39 times smaller than the Earth and the sun is 166 times larger and at a distance of 588 terrestrial diameters. It is difficult to speak of the stars for they are so far away that a stone thrown from one of them, falling at the rate of 74½ milles per hour, would take 100 years to reach the Earth. If a man were to walk at a rate of 25 milles every day, it would take him 7,157½ years to arrive at the stars. Thus, if Adam had started the journey on the day he was born, he would still need to walk for another 713 years from this year of 1245 and would arrive in spring or autumn of 1958. Gossuin is able to be precise in these figures for Christ was born 5,199½ years after the creation of the world.

Then, with that brave attempt to measure the immeasurable which is a hall-mark of his day, Gossuin tries to illustrate the size of the firmament. If there were 100,000 times more people in the world than there are; and if each were a giant and each engendered another every day for 100,000 years; and if each had his castle as large as the king's, with all the lands there attached, and if each had 100 manors each of which held 20 others in fitting state — then there would yet be space for more in the firmament.

And, even as Hell is a locality, so is Heaven, and a good soul may come to it in under half-an-hour's travel. Here, at about the limits of vision of even that most excellent and ingenious viewing instrument devised by King Tolomeus: here, beyond the blue heaven and the crystal heaven, is the purple heaven called imperial. This is the seat of God and His angels, and the description of its glories fails even Gossuin and the mighty clerks who have guided him from Lorraine to Hell via Taprobane and the Islands of the Sea.

Unlike the great Italian vision of Inferno and Paradise created a generation later, Gossuin's view of Creation is pedestrian. He was an encyclopedist primarily and a poet only secondarily and the world as he saw it was as the world his fellows saw. The intellectual forces of enquiry were employed in the fields of theology and philosophy, the exploration of the physical world being left to the magician and the moralist. Nowhere is this more clearly demonstrated than in those bestiaries which were being produced in increasing numbers at about his time. Their purpose was twofold: to give some account of an actual animal and to draw a moral from it. The moral purpose predominated, even though it implied the stretching of a characteristic into unrecognisable form, and employed a kind of circular argument in which a purely symbolic meaning became a supposedly real characteristic, thus providing more symbols. The breath of the panther is so sweet that it attracts all animals in the forest: in this it is like Christ whose sweetness attracts all men. The religious interpretation buttressed the imaginary characteristic until the existence of the sweet breath of the panther is proved by the fact that it resembles Christ. The evidence of the few men who might have had the leisure to smell the breath of an actual panther would have done little to weaken such a chain of logic.

The intention to develop a parable leads the writers into some curious byways where the symbolic nature of the animal is totally at variance with its true nature. The hedgehog, a harmless enough creature, is typecast as the Devil because, at the time of the grape harvest, the animal shakes the vines and impales the fallen grapes upon its spines. So does the Devil impale the souls of men at the harvest of death and bear them away. Similarly the lion is not the obvious choice of animal to represent Christ, the Lamb of God. But the lion is the king of beasts and therefore it is deemed to resemble Christ the Judge and its every characteristic is dissected and expanded in parable. Its square, solid front and slim flanks are symbols of the divine and human characteristics of Christ. Its great claws are to take vengeance upon the Jew — shown in the accompanying illustration as an ass. It effaces its track with its tail — a symbol of the incarnation when God, to cheat the Devil, became man in secret.

Even as the most obscure symbolism is unearthed, the most obvious discrepancies pass unnoticed. The unicorn can be caught only by a virgin who bares her breast. The unicorn is God, the virgin is Mary and her bared breast the manifest Church. The curious implications of the parable — that man is the hunter, God the hunted and that the Deity became

71

incarnate after the Christian Church was founded — are all acceptable in the homiletic cause. Some of the zoological characteristics have obvious if colourful applications. The beaver which severs its testicles in order to escape the hunter is an admirable example for those holy hermits who would triumph over temptation. So too is the ostrich which hides in the sand each year on the rising of a certain star, forgetting its eggs: on the rising of the celestial star of faith the holy man abandons home and family and seeks the desert. The fornicator is urged to consider the fate of the antelope. This shy and chaste beast does not seem to be the most obvious symbol for this kind of sin: but it uses its needle sharp horns to scythe down trees and the hunter captures it when it entangles its horns in a bush. In this it is like man to whom God has given two horns, the Old and New Testaments with which to scythe down the trees of sin. Women, however, form a snare in which he can entangle himself and the Infernal Hunter then captures him. The plover has the power to cure the sick by its glance but will turn its head away if they are afflicted by an incurable illness. This is another symbol for Christ, who turns his eye away from the Jew.

The Cult of the Saint

Theoretically belonging to a universal Church even as they belonged to a universal Empire, men nevertheless looked to the local church as the centre of their religious life even as they looked to the local lord as the centre of their political life. The Church, of its nature, created an internationalism of learning and of administration and of the forms of worship: but it could not eradicate the intense localism which, born of the absence of communication, was ratified by the feudal structure of society. Rome, for most, was an echo on the other side of the world, its activities scarcely to be distinguished from those of the mythical city of antiquity. The local church was Christianity made tangible, and the relics of holy men deposited in local shrines meant more than the whole ghostly empire of theology. A wise man, indeed, ensured that a partner to a contract reinforced an oath taken upon the Gospels with one taken on the relics of the local saint.

The complex dogma of the Christian Church regarding the heavenly hierarchy inevitably found day-to-day expression in something virtually indistinguishable from polytheism. Scholars might make careful distinction between *dulia*, the honour paid to the saints, and *latria*, the worship due to God alone, but such distinction became easily blurred in practice. In order to find expression for the extraordinary place occupied by the Virgin Mary, the term *hyperdulia* was coined — honour higher than that accorded to the saints, worship less than that accorded to God: it was asking much of an unlettered people to bear this limitation in mind when praying for favours. To a people already conditioned to the acceptance of the miraculous as an element of the mundane, such a limitation was in any case unnecessary. The spiritual world shaded into the physical without clear-cut boundary: there could be no clear distinction between such a supposedly natural creature as the phoenix, with its power to pass in and out of the Other World, and the supernatural spirit which entered the natural world to guide or torment. The marvels attributed to beasts and men of distant lands were of the same order as the miracles attributed to saints nearer home.

The most indefatigable transformer of folk-tale into miracle in all France, if not all Europe, was undoubtedly Gregory of Tours. Bishop of Clermont and then of Tours during the murderous chaos of the sixth century, he discharged his dangerous office with courage and skill — and also found time to write two books which, in their differing ways, had a profound influence. His *Historia Francorum* was written to record 'the wars of kings with hostile nations, of martyrs with pagans, of churches with heretics', and, for all its declared bias, formed a source of such authority as to earn for its writer the title of Father of French History. His other book, *De Miraculis*, took the element of Christian propaganda to extreme lengths. It was a labour of love, for he worked at it over the greater part of his life, unwilling, it seemed, to bring his work to a close when every journey he undertook on affairs of state could also result in the discovery of new miracles. Later hagiographers treated *De Miraculis* as a God-sent gift to enrich the products of their own imagination, endlessly repeating those 'miracles' to which Gregory, so hard-headed in political matters, so credulous in religious, gave the weight of his great authority. The numbers of miracles increased not only with the increasing number of saints but with the attempts of hagiographers to shore up a rapidly devaluing currency. The raising of dead men now was a commonplace; walking on water or endowing the brute creation with speech ranked little higher than causing rain or ending strife. A few sceptics, otherwise deeply religious, deplored the undignified multiplication of marvellous stories and their dangerous corollary — the worship of relics. Guibert of Nogent made the attempt with his scathing *Of the Souvenirs of Saints* — an examination both of the claims to sanctity of a dubious regiment of local saints and of the efficacy of their relics. He was well suited to the task, being deeply read in both sacred and secular literature and able to achieve an attractive balance in his own books. He himself was many times asked to write the life of this or that saint but always declined. 'I may be deceived regarding what I actually witnessed. How, then, can I speak truly about that which nobody ever saw?' The speed with which a cult could develop, totally obscuring its origins, was well illustrated by the story of the little boy who, within living memory, had happened to die upon a Good Friday. Impressed by the coincidence, his neighbours began to visit his grave, others followed and soon a minor, unofficial saint complete with his own miracles was in existence. Another holy man whose past Guibert took the trouble to unravel turned out to be a notorious drunkard who had accidentally drowned himself while in his cups.

If the grave of an unknown small boy could attract streams of pilgrims then the shrine of a great saint could become the scene of unseemly violence. Abbot Suger of St-Denis vividly described the fearful pressure of people who came to view the relic of the patron saint of France.

> Those who entered [the church] could not get out and strove in vain against the crowd at the doors. Within the church no one could walk; women were pressed as in a winepress, shrieked as though in childbirth. Many were carried out with extreme difficulty to the monks' meadow but expired there. Others, to escape death, walked on the heads of men as on a continuous floor. The religious who showed the relics were so crowded that more than once they were obliged to escape by the windows with their precious burden.

A generation after Suger wrote his account there was a first-class scandal about this same great relic. The priests of St-Étienne produced what they claimed to be the real head of St Denis. The men of St-Denis, to prove their case, were forced to open the silver box in which the saint's headless body reposed. It disposed of the impious claim of their rivals but could not destroy the grave and growing suspicion that this body was not that of the great Denis the Areopagite who had

75

been converted by St Paul, but that of a humble if virtuous Gallo-Roman. Peter Abelard was foolish enough to query the illustrious antecedents of this famous relic while he was a guest in St-Denis and was in consequence driven out. But a few years later his scepticism was justified when, in 1216, the unimpeachable corpse of the Areopagite was discovered still in its tomb in distant Greece. Innocent III thought it discreet not to offend the powerful monks of St-Denis and their patron the king, whose ancestors reposed in the abbey. He merely forwarded the remains saying, in effect, that now that they had two attested corpses, one of them must indubitably be that of the Areopagite.

The long controversy over the authenticity of the remains of St Denis was founded as much on a lively appreciation of its financial value, as on a pious desire to prove possession of one of the great saints of France. The relic of a famous saint drew crowds of pilgrims and could turn an unknown sanctuary into a powerful and wealthy monastery. The remains of a certain Austremoine, 'the apostle of the Auvergne', had lain in Mozac for over 500 years with great benefit to that community. But when the priests of nearby Issoire put out a strong claim that they possessed the authentic relic, Mozac went into a swift decline as the crowds of pilgrims transferred their devotions and their alms to Issoire. So grave was the situation in which the community found itself that it demanded an episcopal enquiry. It was conclusively proved that Mozac held the true remains and the usurping men of Issoire sank back into their obscurity. The Mozac sanctuary was unusually fortunate in that it possessed documentary proof of the genuineness of its relic. Most monasteries relied upon their resident hagiographers to evolve a history for their relic which would cover satisfactorily the gap, of perhaps centuries, which existed between a living person and his relic. The discovery of one relic would lead to the discovery of others in its class. The first definite record of the Holy Coat of Trèves is that of 1106. For 50 years it enjoyed its unique status and then divine revelation disclosed that a similar relic — the robe made for the Holy Child by his mother — was to be found at Argenteuil. The Empress Irene had sent it to Charlemagne who had given it to Argenteuil and it had been 'forgotten' to be remembered, presumably, only after the Holy Coat had proved its immense popularity.

Guibert particularly deplored the trade in relics. It was common knowledge that there were sufficient fragments of the True Cross to assemble several crosses. The practitioners claimed, on the highest authority, that holy relics had the power of reproducing themselves, of sharing that ability of the Host to be forever divided and yet forever retain its potency. Nevertheless, Guibert maintained, it was ludicrous that there should be two heads of St John the Baptist in existence. Other and weightier condemnations than Guibert's were made. The Council of Poitiers forbade the use of relics as articles of trade and the Lateran Council itself made emphatic statements that the right of acceptance of a new relic belonged to Rome alone. But it was impossible to prevent some venerated object from gaining a local recognition, impossible too to persuade its custodians of an error possibly sanctified by centuries. The Bishop of Orleans protested angrily at the ceremonial that attended the discovery of the lost head of St Geneviève, accusing its custodians of substituting the head of an obscure old woman for that of the saint's. The prior of St-Geneviève denied it, and offered to put the matter to the test by walking through fire with it. The undignified argument was ended only when the archbishop of Sens commanded his bishop to silence, implicitly condemning his scepticism. In the absence of documentation, proof of such a matter was, in any case, an act of faith as Guibert pointed out regretfully.

Around the Host, the relic of Christ himself, there grew a vast body of legends. In vain Thomas Aquinas insisted that transubstantiation was an invisible miracle, that any vision of actual change from bread to flesh could lie only in the mind of the beholder. Guibert, so sceptical about saintly relics, nevertheless recorded with approval the vision of the little child who saw the bread change into the body of a boy on Easter Day. This vision of a child appearing on the altar at the moment of consecration was a common one and, when linked to the complete ritual of consecration, produced an horrific vision in which the priest was seen to rend the body of a boy during the breaking of bread. The bread sometimes changed to flesh to confound a sceptical priest. One such piece of blood-suffused flesh was long kept as a relic which attracted crowds of pilgrims. St Louis declined to turn aside and visit the sanctuary where it was kept, saying that such miracles were needed only for the infirm of faith. Jacques de Vitry tells the story of an evil priest who kept the Host in his mouth after communicating, intending to use it as a love philtre. Appalled by its effect upon his body he hid it, confessed his sin, and returned to restore it to the altar. It had changed to a crucifix of flesh and blood.

The growing cult of the Virgin Mary, which opponents of later generations were to describe as mariolatry, received a powerful impetus in 1140 when the canons of Lyons introduced the Festival of the Immaculate Conception. There were high and honourable names among the ranks of those who opposed the innovation. Not only the suspect Abelard but also the unimpeachable Bernard of Clairvaux fought vigorously against that growing belief in the immaculate

78

conception of Mary which virtually removed her from the ranks of human beings. 'How can this be?' Bernard demanded of the priests of Lyons. If she were indeed born free of original sin, then so must each of her thousands of ancestors, 'since otherwise she could not have descended from them worthily and there would then be festivals without number'. Aquinas followed Bernard but popular opinion totally ignored this austere interpretation and, finding champions among other scholars, the belief was ultimately proclaimed an article of faith. One of Bernard's own monks had a vision of him in which he appeared, after death, with a single stain on his otherwise spotless soul — a stain caused by his refusal to accept the belief. Bernard was, in spite of this opposition, a fervent champion of the Virgin as the Mediatrix. Guibert explained the complex argument, whereby the created can influence the judgements of the creator, by a homely analogy. The Virgin was the Mother of God and 'a mother does not pray — she orders. This is why Christ listens and can be persuaded to change his judgements.'

But the subtle arguments of scholars were coarsened into a practice in which it is impossible to see any distinction drawn between Mary, the woman honoured above all mortal humans, and the Madonna, worshipped as the unchanging female element in religion. The sum of the countless *fabliaux* in which she figures is the demonstration of her unqualified power to help those who accord her honour — even though their lives or their requests are morally dubious. A robber who had always prayed to her before going forth on his murderous expeditions was caught and condemned. She supported his feet in the gallows and, when the executioner tried to despatch him with a sword, she deflected the blade. A story with endless variations is that of the nun who absconds with a lover. Returning to her nunnery after many years she finds that her absence has gone unnoticed, for the Virgin — to whom she had always paid devotion — had taken her place. A wife demands vengeance upon her lover's other mistress. The Virgin professes herself incapable of helping, because the woman 'bows before my image too times a day'. A man is prepared to renounce God and all his saints to obtain the love of a woman but declines to renounce the Virgin. His tempter refuses to help him but she, at this evidence that the man holds her in greater honour than he does God, grants him his request. In the songs of the troubadours the Virgin as defender of lovers becomes herself very close to being an object of physical love. In these *chansons* the change from *hyperdulia* to pagan worship is complete and the Mother of God undergoes the final transformation to emerge as that older figure, the Goddess of Love.

4: ART AND ARCHITECTURE

Building of the Cathedrals

As though in response to the sense of universal relief that the world had again been spared, that the year 1000 did not mark the Second Coming, there began a tremendous renewal of religious architecture shortly after the turn of the millennium. 'It seemed as though all the world were throwing off its slumber to clothe itself anew in an array of white sanctuaries', a contemporary recorded. 'People everywhere began to restore the churches, and, though many of them were still in good condition, they vied with each other in erecting new buildings, one more beautiful than the other.'

The new architecture was strongly reminiscent of the old, for the models were Roman. A century and more was to pass before certain daring men in the Île de France, experimenting with the structure of the arch, brought about the fantasy of Gothic, the architectural expression of the north. The new churches springing up in the south were adaptations of the ancient basilica, and Provence provided models as classically pure as any in Italy. The Romanesque style underlined the fact that this vast land mass was still not yet a nation. The products of architecture, being intended only for the people of the locality, exactly reflects the society that gives it birth. 'France' was still merely an area around the city of Paris and the styles of Romanesque differed as greatly from one province to another as it differed from country to country. There was, indeed, closer affinity between the buildings of Normandy and England than between those of Normandy and any other area in France.

It is sometimes possible to trace the development of Romanesque architecture through the movements of one architect. Such a one was Abbot William of Volpiano who, coming from Lombardy, passed into Burgundy and then, at the request of Duke Richard II, went to Normandy to assist the monks there, 'giving no slight assistance by his advice in laying foundations'. It was through him that the new style developed in Normandy and thence in England, although the Normans, ever quick to learn, gave it their own characteristic features. Burgundy, the cradle of that monasticism which was the driving force behind the resurgence, took the massive legacy of Rome and transmuted it. The round vault and the round arch were retained, together with the enormous walls which they demanded, but the height was raised, beginning the aspiration which found its culmination in Gothic. The Minster of the great Benedictine house at Cluny was rebuilt between 1089 and 1131 in a fashion fitting the mother-house of the most powerful religious Order in Europe. It became the largest church outside Italy, with its five naves and five towers. The monastery itself had to contain within its compass everything that a human being might need to work, live and eat, for Benedict had enjoined that a monk's life should be spent within the precincts. Around the Minster therefore grew the humbler buildings necessary for a community: brewery and bakehouse, dormitory, lavatory, workshops of every kind from those of the glaziers and goldsmiths to those of the scribes and blacksmiths. Benedictine rule emphasised the sanctity of manual labour and the monks therefore built their own monastery and church, assembling thereby a corpus of architectural knowledge, reducing problems to sets of laws, which their brethren, working perhaps hundreds of miles distant, could copy. Cluny and its daughter-houses of Cîteaux and Clairvaux were the inspiration for scores of identical foundations throughout Europe: by the eleventh century 314 monasteries were in the obedience, each built according to the standard laid down by the mother-foundation.

Sometime about the middle of the twelfth century an anonymous group of men working somewhere in the lie de France produced the revolutionarily simple design of the pointed arch. It is possible that this pointed arch developed in response to the desire to enlarge the window areas: the Bishops of Cambrai and Auxerre both, independently, ordered that the existing windows of the cathedrals should be enlarged. More probably, the pointed arch came about as part of a logical sequence in which reduction of weight was sought in order to increase height. The Romanesque builders had overcome the limitation of the barrel-vault by developing the cross-vault: the substitution of panels of lighter masonry in the four triangular panels was a natural development and the entire weight of the vault thus rested on ribs. But these in their turn still required massive, almost windowless, walls to support them: the builders were still limited to the concept of orders rising one upon the other in order to achieve height — massive, enduring, but still essentially earthbound. The pointed arch took the weight of the vault straight down to be supported by buttresses. It was as though sections had been cut out of the wall and placed at right angles to it, eliminating the appearance of solidity so that the building seemed to be soaring upwards, weightless.

The pointed arch appeared at much the same time all over Europe, but it was in France that the architects took the three components — buttress, arch and window — and made of them that style called Gothic. Contemporaries recognised it as being indigenous to France: '*opus francigenum*' the Germans called it when introducing it into their own country. Destined to find its full flowering in the cathedrals, monuments of the secular age, it was nevertheless a monk, Abbot Suger, who first assembled the elements of Gothic into one harmonious whole.

Abbot Suger would have been a rare person in any age, combining as he did the ability to move in two worlds at once. Minister of State by force of circumstances, priest by conviction, he was an ascetic who was also a lively companion; given to enormous enthusiasms, he was yet capable of controlling them. His origins were humble but his great learning took him up the ladder of ecclesiastic preferment which was accessible to all, and he became the most trusted councillor of Louis VI, and then of his son Louis VII. Suger did what he could to ease the scandalous discord between the wretched Louis and his gay Eleanor but, in spite of his own natural gaiety of temperament, he stood for all that Eleanor most disliked in her husband's court.

Suger began the great task of rebuilding the abbey of St-Denis under Louis VI, recording every aspect of the work, its difficulties and triumphs, in a vivid account which has an almost boyish excitement about it. The abbey could almost have been a model to show the successive stages of architectural development in France. Romanesque is still evident, both in arches and decoration; Suger also deliberately used mosaic here and there, although well aware that it was old-fashioned. He ran into difficulties with the construction of the towering new arches, and breathlessly tells of the night of storm when it seemed that his work would come tumbling down — but the new arch stood the test. Stone and glass were brought together in a unique combination: sculptors under the new influence found themselves breaking free of the dignified but stiff Romanesque forms: glaziers experimented with areas of glass huge compared with what had gone before. The result was a glowing jewel of a place fitted to be the repository of the remains of St Denis, the royal abbey of France. Even St Bernard, suspicious of all that smacked of earthly beauty, was impressed. 'This man builds for God alone.'

It is possible that Suger built St-Denis in the new manner to demonstrate that monasticism could keep abreast of the times both physically and spiritually. But the glory was to pass to the secular cathedrals. Romanesque architecture was essentially the expression of monasticism. The vast, massive buildings that rose all over the land between the eleventh and twelfth centuries were built by and for enclosed communities of men, reflecting the power of the abbots who were exempt from all local control. The Gothic cathedral reflected the world outside.

Its development coincided with two great national movements, the growth of the central power under the monarchy and the growth of the towns. In the 43 years of the reign of Philip Augustus, from the years 1180 to 1223, 16 of the great cathedrals of France were begun, including those of Paris, Chartres, Bayeux, Rheims. They were expressions of the popular will, even as the monasteries had been expressions of a religious discipline. Nobles and peasants alike contributed both labour and money. During the rebuilding of Chartres after its disastrous fire, 'there were seen for the first time the faithful harnessing themselves to wagons that were laden with stones, wood, provisions and whatever else was needed for the works of the cathedral. As by the might of magic its towers rose to heaven.' Contemporaries accepted, posterity marvelled, that over the incredibly variegated forms of the cathedrals an essential unity was preserved. In terms of labour, the cathedrals are comparable only with the pyramids of Egypt, but there the severe geometric forms rendered overall control relatively simple. The Gothic cathedral resembles an organic growth, for the parts, rioting in individual exuberance though they were, remained subordinate to the whole. Nothing is more astonishing than that visible ageing of floral motifs which marks the passing of centuries. The earliest cathedrals show leaves and flowers in bud: those of the thirteenth century show them in full flower and those of the fourteenth century show them as autumnal. Even allowing for the fact that the cathedrals were built by a comparatively small number of itinerant master-builders, the prevalence of this unimportant motif over wide areas, changing simultaneously over 200 years, is weirdly impressive. The names of the master-builders have survived, but most are merely names — Pierre de Montreuil who designed St-Denis for Suger, William of Sens who built the cathedral in that city, Jean Langlois who designed that of Troyes, Jean de Chelles that of Paris — little is known of them save their names in the account rolls. Their features might survive anonymously in a detail of minor statuary: few were as fortunate as Libergier, the master-mason of Rheims, whose elaborate tombstone bore his portrait and his name. These were the men who, in wooden shacks grouped around the rising structure, subordinated the parts to the whole.

The master-mason or builder was, in a very real sense, the master, for he combined the functions of architect, contractor, structural and mechanical engineer. He knew nothing of solid geometry, of plans, blueprints, isometric drawings or any of the technical aids which the most humble builder of today instinctively draws upon. He posed and solved his problems in three-dimensional terms, making exquisitely accurate models for each part of the structure as work proceeded. His great problem was not labour, of which there was an abundance, but materials. The quarrying, shaping and transporting of the thousands of tons of stone required was a major operation, the responsibility for which lay at higher levels. Here the king would grant access to royal quarries; there the bishop, or some local lord desirous of obtaining heavenly merit, would arrange for the supply of stone. A less obvious need, but one as vital, was the scores of thousands of feet of timber required for scaffolding and the frames for construction of arches and vaults. Later, builders would make a kind of cradle of the scaffold and erect their building with it. The master-builder of a cathedral would have bankrupted himself before work started if this system had been adopted. The cathedral raised itself up on its own bootstraps. Scaffolding was built up to a certain height and then, when the wall reached that height, the scaffold would be dismantled and re-erected on the wall itself, taking advantage of pre-arranged projections. The galleries that were built into the structure itself, in anticipation of the never-ending task of inspection and maintenance, also discharged the function of scaffolding during construction.

Economy dictated that much of the building should be pre-fabricated. Stone was shaped in the quarries; the great beams were notched and made ready on the ground before being hoisted into place by windlass and pulley. Somewhere in the roof would be set the great wheel which discharged the function of a crane. Lacking the horizontal arm of a crane, it could operate only on a radius of a few feet and had to be shifted every so often as the structure lengthened. But no pre-fabrication could solve the problem of the length of time mortar took to set. The period sometimes ran into months. A too-impatient builder could cause the collapse of the great vault: the roof of many cathedrals show here and there the tell-tale sag where the builder had removed the supporting framework before the mortar had completely set. The vault was constructed in sections, the massive framework being eased forward a little at a time. Jammed against the roof as it was by its function, and enclosed by the projecting ribs of the vaults, the removal of the framework was a difficult operation. One of the methods adopted was to stand the legs in drums of sand while the frame was being built. Plugs were pulled out of the drums when it was required to move the frame and, as the level of the sand fell in the drum, so the whole structure descended until it was clear of the ribs.

The greatest single skill that the master-builder had to develop was, perhaps, the art of delegation. Most of the great cathedrals were finished within a generation: Notre-Dame in Paris, commenced in 1168, was completed by 1220. It would have been impossible for any one man — or even a committee — to approve each detail of the cathedral as it came into existence. The major sculptures alone could run into thousands and apart from these were the innumerable casual touches which made of the building a living creation, an expression of the society that created it. The vast wealth of detail, executed independently by scores of men yet still within an overall discipline, was possible because each member of a gang of workmen was an artist in his own right, capable of following his own path within an overall design. No distinction was drawn between artist and craftsman. The man who sculpted the great Christ of Amiens and the man who squared a block of stone were alike known as masons.

Iconography

Behind the exuberant detail, behind the personal expressions made in stone or glass by mason or glazier, there lay an intellectual plan for a specific purpose. 'Simple and unlettered souls find in the church what they cannot know through books', the Synod of Arras pronounced. 'They see it in the plan.' The cathedral was, quite literally, the Bible of the poor. The wealthy had their Books of Hours in which God's plan for man was shown in gold and lapis-lazuli: for the poor, the blaze of painted glass, the endless ranks of three-dimensional stone pictures performed the same task.

The central symbols of the Christian Church retain their potency even into the present century. The most casual, most irreligious tourist is well aware of the significance of the cruciform shape of church or cathedral. The dominant figures of the Christian faith are immediately and permanently identifiable: Christ cannot be mistaken among a group of figures; Peter will be recognised by his keys; the significance of Madonna and Child will remain unchanged so long as Christianity endures. From the Old Testament the symbols of creation — Adam, Eve, tree, serpent — remain as familiar in significance as the symbols of traffic lights or advertisement. And around these central symbols lie scattered other figures — minor or even mythical — which retain a recognised identity through some quirk of popularity: Jonah and the whale, St Christopher, Noah. But these symbols that remain are merely the topmost leaves of a forest, the bulk of which is now unidentifiable.

Medieval iconography is a vast subject, in both its remains and its implications, for the tiniest church and the greatest cathedral alike have their carvings, each with its specific meanings. An attempt to view the field as a whole would weary the eye, fuddle the brain and occupy years. But there is one unique building, the cathedral of Chartres, which sums up the multifarious forms, gives them order and shows their development. There are some 10,000 carvings of men and animals and plants — a riot of detail to the casual eye, yet, following a definite order imposed upon them by architectonic requirements, they provide now a three-dimensional textbook as once they provided a Bible.

The cathedral stands on a little hill in the middle of a great plain so that, effortlessly, it dominates, the city falling away below it like the skirts of a robe. It had an unfortunate genesis, being twice destroyed by fire. The disaster of 1134 precipitated an astounding demonstration of popular enthusiasm when nobles and people alike laboured together to rebuild it. Scarcely had the work been completed when, in 1194, another fire destroyed all save the towers and west front. With an incredible resilience the citizens again rallied to their cathedral. The west front was moved forward to line up with the towers and the north and south porches replanned. Sixty years later the work was completed, the new sculptures for the porches being finished in 1280.

The accident of fire has provided an unusual insight into the changing methods and ideals of a vital period. A century separates the sculptures of the west front from those of the north and south porches. Both groups of sculptors were working with the same end in view, subordinating their work to the overall design of the same cathedral: the differences in their technique are therefore born of their own subconscious differences, and chart the intellectual path traversed over two generations. The west front is still Romanesque and the figures upon it are conventional: the faces show great strength and dignity but they are portraits of the species, not the individual; of justice, not of a judge; of Eve, not of a woman. The sculptures of the north and south porches show a delicacy and an individuality — the awareness of human identity which has already found its way into the scholar's study. There can be no greater contrast between the great Christ of the royal door of the west front — withdrawn, remote — with the gentle, almost feminine Christ of the south porch. The change is shown even in the matter of decoration, for in the west front it is conventional while in the north and south porches it takes the form of living wreaths of flowers — buttercups, ivy, columbine, tenderly winding within the geometric discipline.

The sculptors were faced with the problem of telling a series of stories over a number of changing surfaces. There were in all nine sets of tympana, arches, lintels, capitals, plinths and pillars, and each class of surface was devoted to a particular story. Like the chapters of a book, each of the portals was devoted to a single main theme — in the west, the glorification of Christ; in the dark north, the story of the Old Testament; in the sunlit south, the saints and the Last Judgement. Christ and his mother occupy the place of honour, the curved tympanum, while saints and prophets guard the doors as pillars. The identities of those on the west front are now obscure: to the people who built the cathedral and to their children these superhuman figures would have been as familiar as members of their family.

The blocks of the statues were carved in workshops — a departure from the older method of carving on the site — each motif starting and ending with a block. Over the arches are displayed the signs of the Zodiac, but intermixed with these symbols of an ancient world are the homely pictures symbolising the labours of the month, the sculptor placing beside the Babylonian Crab or Scales the figure of his own neighbour pursuing his daily work in a French field. The labours of the months follow the same design as is used in the Books of Hours: January is a two-headed god drinking wine; February is an old man huddled over a fire; March is the time for steeping flax; April shows vine pruning. Details are executed with the care and knowledge born of unthinking familiarity. The harvest shown in the south porch is later than that shown in the north porch — a man from the colder north possibly executed this. The fire under the pot of lead in which St Vitus is enduring martyrdom is being carefully blown by a very practical pair of bellows. Here and there is evidence of hurry, of lack of care or skill. One wonders how the head of St John — a weak, almost idiotic face with gaping mouth — passed both the master-builder and the cathedral authorities. The probability is that they never saw it among the thousands of sculptures being produced. The dragon upon which the saint stands is executed with verve, the sculptor seeming more at home with mythical monster than holy saint.

Seen from a distance, the cathedral seems bare to the point of austerity. Close too, and these porches of Chartres display a catechism within their exuberance. The unknown masons and their hundreds of fellows scattered over the land did their work well. Five hundred years after the Synod of Arras made its learned pronouncement, Francois Villon, thief and poet, placed in the mouth of his illiterate mother words that explained the years of loving labour spent upon stone and glass and wood. 'I am a poor, old woman who knows nothing, who cannot read. But in the church I see Paradise painted, and Hell where the damned broil.'

Stained Glass

The towering, glowing pictures in living colour that made an art form of the practical need to introduce light into a building was a unique gift of medieval Christianity to the art of the world. The use of coloured glass in windows was very ancient, but the combining of the two mediums of glass and enamel arose some time in the tenth century and reached its peak in the fifteenth century. Theophilus, the twelfth-century monkish writer on art, specifically referred to glass-painting as being French in origin and certainly, from an early period, identifiable schools of French glass-painters drew a luminous trail across Europe. The men who worked for Abbot Suger went on to Chartres, then to Angers and finally to York to create the great windows of the Minster. Five hundred years earlier, the Venerable Bede had recorded that Benedict Biscop, Abbot of Monkswearmouth, 'sent messengers to Gaul to fetch makers of glass till then unknown in England', and a few years later, in 709, Bishop Wilfrid of York repeated the invitation. But these 'workers in glass windows' were glass-makers; the trail of the glass-painters leads to Limoges where, in 979, a colony of Venetian mosaic-workers had settled. They developed there the form of enamel-work known as *cloisonné*, in which strips of metal separate the areas to be filled with coloured enamel. The two techniques — the enamelling and the system of dividing the areas — were the effective origins of the art.

The glass used was a special toughened substance which, for the greater part of its history, was produced in kilns in open country. The French called such glass *'verre de fougère'*, referring to the bracken or fern that was burnt to provide the necessary alkali. In England, the relationship between *fougère* and *forêt* became confused and the glass was known as 'forest glass'. In its early period it was far from perfect, but these very imperfections increased the richness of the finished product as the light was deflected by the various angles of the imperfections. The colours were limited to the primaries and their composites — blue, red, yellow, green — and were produced by introducing various metals into the molten glass. The colours were called by the name of the precious stone which they most nearly resembled, red becoming ruby, green becoming emerald, blue becoming sapphire, a nomenclature still internationally adopted in the trade.

Theophilus describes in considerable detail the method of preparing a stained-glass window. A large, smooth board was whitewashed with a mixture of chalk and water which then set into a glaze. Upon this the design was traced, the different colours required being marked by letters. Sections of glass of the required colours were placed over the relevant parts of the design, the outlines traced and then the glass cut to shape, using a hot iron. The loose pieces of glass were then assembled and, upon this mosaic of coloured glass, the picture was painted.

The black or brown enamel which was used, though dull in itself, drew the coloured segments of glass into an intellectual whole. The process of enamelling which Theophilus describes was that developed by the Limoges artists. To prepare the enamel itself 'take copper beaten small, burn it in a little pipkin until it is entirely pulverised, then take pieces of green glass and sapphire paste and pound them separately between porphyry stones. Mix these ingredients together in the form of one-third green glass, one-third copper powder, one-third sapphire paste. Grind them on the same stone with wine or urine and paint the glass with the utmost care.' Theophilus claimed that 'if you are diligent with the work, you can make the lights and shadows of draperies and of the human face in the same manner as in a coloured painting.' The monochrome painting thus executed came to life when light passed through the glass, blending enamel and coloured glass into a whole. Dark lines had to be solid and heavy to stand up against the blaze of light; fingers were separated from each other by bands of enamel as thick as a finger itself. After the painting, the glass was returned to the kiln when the enamel was fused on.

The next stage was that of leading. The artists of later centuries regarded the lead as a necessary nuisance but those of the twelfth and thirteenth centuries employed its potential to the full, seeing it not merely as a device to hold the fragments together but as an intrinsic part of the design, its solid blackness separating colours that would otherwise have mixed and blurred. The glazier used the lead to follow natural contours of body or drapery so that it did not obtrude as a medium.

The ability to design and control huge areas of glass found its supreme expression in the Ste-Chapelle, built between 1245 and 1248 to house the Holy Thorn. At first glance, the interior seems to be composed almost entirely of glass, the massive supporting framework disappearing into the general design. This great area of glass posed a problem which could be satisfactorily solved only by glazier, mason and blacksmith working together in the closest co-operation. Unsupported, the area of glass and soft lead would disintegrate with its own weight: clumsy, obtrusive support would have totally destroyed the careful harmony of the design. The ribs of the roof vaults are brought down in slender columns which divide the total area into narrow rectangles, each of which is further divided by thin stone bars disposed as tracery. Sometimes the supports are deliberately emphasised as in the Crucifixion window at Poitiers. Here the blood-red central cross is outlined by iron supports, the sombre, bold outline heightening the dramatic impact instead of detracting from the pattern.

An ordered classification of subject existed in glass-painting as in sculpture, so that in a particular type of area a particular class of subject will appear. The Last Judgement, Christ, and the Labours of the Months are usually placed in transept and west windows. The Apostles and Prophets dominate the choir, with the eastern chapel dedicated to the life of the Virgin. In the nave aisles, the common people find a place, for these windows were the gift of craft guilds or *métiers*, the members of which will appear at the bottom of the window engaged in their particular craft. So it is that the humble people — carpenters, tanners, bakers — share in the glowing immortality granted to those great ones who appeared as individual donors.

Illumination

The art of the miniaturist had come down from very ancient times, for it had been revived by the Carolingian renaissance. The art declined when the Empire itself disintegrated, but rose again during the renaissance of the twelfth century when, according to Dante, it gained its name of 'illumination' in Paris. It was a romantic but descriptive term: Joinville, speaking of his saintly master Louis, describes him illuminating his kingdom as a scribe illuminates his book with blue and gold.

Until the fourteenth century, the craft was very largely a monastic occupation, carried on particularly in the Benedictine houses. Their standardised *scriptoria* were arranged with a view to something approaching mass-production. Usually, the entire walk of the cloister nearest the church was devoted to *scriptoria* and library. On the inner wall of the cloister were placed the *armaria*, great oaken cupboards supplied with strong locks for the security of the precious manuscripts used as the library. Opposite the cupboards were the little square cubicles called *carrés*, whose name passed into English as 'carrels'. They were floored and roofed with wood yet, placed on the outside wall of a draughty cloister, must have been cold enough and their standard equipment included a brazier. Their average dimensions of six feet by eight made them just large enough to accommodate the scribe, his desk and equipment.

Towards the end of the thirteenth century, secular workers began to infiltrate, their increase coinciding with the trade guilds. Their presence slowly influenced the type of manuscript produced. The movement towards secularisation can be traced from the first daring innovations made in the universal religious subjects, breaking away from the rigid formalism that dictated the colour of the Virgin's robe, the position of the Child, the crib, the angle of the body in a Descent from the Cross. Presentation of subject had been hallowed by a tradition a millennium old, and from this break-away the progress towards purely secular subjects was ensured. The figure of the patron begins to appear, at first minute, tucked away in an inconspicuous corner but then gradually becoming larger until, with the great blaze of the Flemish and Parisian works of the fifteenth century, the miniatures have become formal portraits. Those manuscripts intended for very wealthy patrons maintained the great tradition, but the majority, intended for mass consumption, showed a definite deterioration. There had been no economic pressure upon a monastic worker: an abbot impatiently awaiting a finished work was a far less stringent taskmaster than a patron who had paid out a great deal of money in materials and wanted to see the finished product before his death. Now there was the standing temptation for a lay-worker to skimp details, to cover clumsy execution with a mass of gold — a temptation which few resisted and which contributed slowly but surely to the degradation of the craft.

The artist who prepared his own pigments had to have an elementary knowledge of botany and chemistry, of zoology and geology, for his materials came from every source that would yield a colour. Minerals provided gold, copper, red lead, sulphide of mercury for the brilliant vermilion, marble which was burnt to provide lime for white. The murex shell-fish provided a glorious purple, carmine came from the little ilex beetle. The earth itself provided green (*terra verde*), red ochre, yellow ochre and the sombre colour known as sienna. From vegetables were obtained indigo, cornflower-blue, leek-green, and madder. There sometimes seems to be a touch of sympathetic magic in the choice of materials for certain colours. Jean de Bègue claimed that azure-blue could be made from the pure juice of the cornflower. 'It will need three, four or five layers or more but you will have the colour of azure.' This, and other vegetable extracts, was mixed with powdered chalk to give it body.

The most important, and the most expensive, of the colours was blue. Until a relatively late date it was the mandatory colour for the costume of the Madonna and the only fitting source was lapis-lazuli. The stone was ground and the blue particles extracted by washing; to the initial high cost of the stone was the added expense that only a low proportion of blue powder was obtainable from the precious stone. Ultramarine blue was worth more than double its weight in gold and the usual practice was for the patron to supply it, the illuminator paying for all lesser colours and charging the expense later.

Gold could be used either as a fluid or as a leaf. The first method was the older, and consisted simply of mixing gold-powder with water and size and using it as any other pigment. It was simpler to use than gold leaf but could not take that mirror-like finish which could only be obtained by burnishing gold-leaf. The preparation of the base upon which the gold-leaf was laid was the most complex and most important part of the work. Known as mordant, a basic recipe contained gypsum, white marble and egg-shells, all ground together to a powder and mixed with white of egg. Red ochre or terracotta was added to give colour, guiding the artist when he came to fill in the design traced upon a white parchment. The mordant was applied in thin coats, each of which was allowed to dry and then burnished before the next layer was applied. It was a tedious and lengthy task for each layer took many days to dry but, prepared in this way, a hard, smooth, flexible base was available for the gold-leaf. When ready, white of egg was laid over the base and a leaf of purest gold — thicker than that in use today — was slipped on. Jean de Bègue's simple recipe for the task of burnishing was 'burnish and go on burnishing until the sweat runs down the forehead'. It was no job for a weakling but it was also necessary to be extremely careful. The mordant stood out from the parchment, and it was necessary to work the leaf over the whole curve so that the finished product would resemble a golden button or boss. It was extremely difficult to make a neat edge of the gold and the boss was usually outlined in black to conceal the uneven line.

The austere Cistercian Order forbade the use of gold. St Bernard carried this distrust of ornament to extreme lengths, even questioning the appearance of those grotesque little figures which casually appear in the foliated margins. Yet it was this very limitation of ornament, enforced by religious scruple, that brought about a new and most beautiful decoration, that of grisaille. The work is almost monochrome, executed in a bluish-grey tone with dull, fluid gold being used for the highlights. It relied for its effects not upon the rather gaudy blaze of colour generally employed but in exactness of execution. The better examples resemble a cameo or even a relief.

The growing trend towards secularisation of subject was given a powerful impetus by Philip the Bold, Duke of Burgundy, a great and wealthy patron of the arts. Purely secular manuscripts begin to appear increasingly from the early fourteenth century. The great *chansons* were natural subjects for the illuminators but contemporary writers, too, found their works so honoured, the Chronicles of Froissart being particularly popular. At the same time, Books of Hours were produced on a scale unmatched until the coming of the printing press. Here the principles of mass-production were clearly employed for the cheaper productions: they usually had the same set of illustrations produced on a conveyor belt system where one man would outline, the next apply gold, another pigments.

The most famous of these Books of Hours were commissioned by another prince of the royal blood. Jean, Duke of Berry, was a dilettante who stood aside from the bloody chaos brought upon his country by the Hundred Years War, the madness of the King, and the struggle for power between the regents. A very wealthy man, he was able to indulge his passion for works of art and, amongst the vast number of such objects, commissioned two Books of Hours: that in 1410 known as the *Chantilly* or *Belles Heures* and the *Très Riches Heures* begun by the Limbourg brothers in 1416. Paul and Jean de Limbourg came to Paris from the Netherlands in 1399 and Berry, ever on the look-out for new talent, brought them into his direct service. The brothers were probably responsible for part at least of the *Belles Heures* but the six years that separate the two books show a remarkable change. The *Belles Heures* are concerned still with largely religious subjects: landscape, where it appears, is formal. In the *Très Riches Heures*, the portraits of the Duke and his retainers are but a few degrees removed from a painting, their miniature size alone distinguishing them from ordinary portraits. And in the labours of the months, the brothers go out confidently into the fields and villages. Ploughing, sowing, grape-harvesting, so the life of ordinary people is embalmed in glowing colour. Architecture too finds a place, for towering in the background behind the groups of labourers in each of the illustrations is one of Berry's 20 castles.

And yet, unlike the bolder, simpler earlier products, this work of the Limbourg brothers is removed from reality. The workers in the fields are, after all, musical-comedy peasants, cleansed and clothed to be fit for the eye of a prince of the fleur-de-lis. The haymakers in June are dressed in clean, decorative garments, their tender, pink feet incongruous in the stubble. The women draw up their beautiful blue robes to disclose crisp, white undergarments. A sheep-shearer is portrayed in full court dress complete with flowing robe and hat — in July. The artists capture the brutal, stupid expression of a swineherd — but dress him in cloth of gold. Closer to reality are the nobles themselves whether feasting in January or making love in May. Their brilliant robes echo the brilliance of the flowers as they do in real life: they laugh, sing, hunt, oblivious of the peasants who form a backcloth to their gaudy lives.

5: EDUCATION AND LEARNING

The Grammar Schools

Bernard of Chartres, first of the teachers to found a recognisable school, summed up the achievements of his contemporaries in a sentence at once humble and proud. 'We are but as dwarfs seated upon the shoulders of giants: in this manner we see more than the ancients.' The giants of whom he spoke were the classic authors but he, and all those who came after him, owed as much to the near illiterate Frankish Emperor as they did to any Latin writer. During his gigantic task of refashioning the Empire Charlemagne had seen that without coherent instruction of the young, his Europe would remain a collection of barbaric nations. There already existed the physical means to introduce a system of universal education — the scores of monasteries and cathedrals, most of them richly endowed and with space to spare. He therefore ordered that both types of foundations should maintain schools, the teachers being drawn from the monastery and the cathedral chapter. His own inspectors ensured that a minimum standard was observed and, in this manner, a tincture of knowledge was infused throughout the land. The schools declined with all else after the collapse of the Empire, but the seed was dormant, not dead.

The great Cluniac reform of the eleventh century gave new life to the monastic schools. Yet, of their nature, few could provide anything but a very limited education. The monasteries formed enclosed communities, usually far from the influence — baneful or beneficial — of urban society. The children entrusted to their care were subjected to the same rigorous

102

discipline of the adult monk, in response to the prevailing view of the child as a miniature man. In their prayers and in their bed, at bathing, eating, they were never out of sight of their guardians. Forbidden to talk, to sing, to play, their lives were dedicated to one purpose — the obtaining of that limited knowledge necessary for their later profession as priest. Learning was by rote, the children endlessly chanting the correct responses from the liturgy or the Gospels so that reading became valueless, ousted by the primitive methods of mnemonics. A few of the monastic schools developed into centres of learning equal to any of the cathedral schools. Under Lanfranc, the later Archbishop of Canterbury, the abbey of Bee in Normandy had an international reputation, producing two archbishops of Canterbury, a pope and that Anselm who laid the foundations of Scholasticism. But the majority of monastic schools, conservative and introspective, played little part in the revival of learning. They discharged a valuable function in bringing some form of culture into remote areas but it was in the cathedral schools that the future of learning lay.

The child enrolled in a cathedral school also found himself in a totally adult world. There was no attempt to equate age with subjects taught, or to separate age groups into classes. All the students of a school, whether grown men of 20 or little boys of eight, shared the same, single room and were engaged in the same cycle of studies. The sacred Seven Arts formed the whole corpus of knowledge and were divided into two main sections: the *Trivium* — grammar, rhetoric, logic — and the *Quadrivium* — arithmetic, geometry, astronomy and music. The *Trivium* dominated in the earlier period; the study of the *Quadrivium* reflected the beginning of the preoccupation with pure science in the thirteenth century. Grammar was the bedrock of the

Trivium and thence of all scholarship, and the student's first book — and one which many carried throughout their career — was the Donat. Thus, simply, was known the *Ars grammatica* of Aelius Donatus, a fourth-century grammarian who had taught St Jerome in Rome. His book survived the debacle of the classic Empire to become the main textbook of medieval education — so much so, that *donat* became the synonym for any elementary treatise on any subject. Grammar meant Latin grammar only and around and round its every part, for year after year, the student plodded. Curiously, though the grammar of this one language was studied to excess, languages themselves were almost totally ignored. It was, perhaps, a natural result of the fragmented nature of society: a man would need to know not merely French, or Italian, or German but half-a-dozen dialects in each tongue, each with the status of a language. The Duke of Nevers boasted that among the foreign languages he spoke were French, Norman and Poitevin. But the dominance of Latin to the exclusion of all languages in the syllabus also demonstrated the closed circle of education. The master in his high place would read from one of a very few set authors, commenting upon the construction, examining the meaning according to a rigid formula. He would then receive back from his students what he had given out, reflected for the most part unthinkingly.

The character of the little school depended totally upon the master. In time, in those cathedral schools which would develop into universities, the number of masters increased, bringing specialisation. But in the earlier years of the eleventh century, and in all the smaller schools, one or two masters taught all subjects. The poorer among them taught in the open streets, setting up their meagre stock-in-trade at a crossroad. Those who could afford it would rent a room which was little more than a barn. There would be straw upon the floor to give some slight warmth in winter and to absorb the more liquid filth. In Paris the Rue du Fouarre — Street of Straw — became a synonym for the embryonic university. Of furniture there was very little: a high stool for the master himself, possibly a lectern if he could afford it and that was all. The students themselves sat upon the floor, for it was not until the late fourteenth century that the luxury of even a few wooden benches was provided. And, having obtained his licence to teach from the chancellor of the chapter, and bought his stool and hired his room, the master would wait spider-like until a student, bored with his present master or unable to find a place with a popular man, came to him.

The University of Paris

'The Grand Pont is the centre of things, crowded with goods, merchants, boats. The Petit Pont is taken over by the dialecticians, walking to and fro, discussing the nature of things. In the Île, adjoining the palace of the king, one sees the palace of philosophy where learning reigns supreme, the citadel of light and immortality, the eternal dwelling of the Seven Sisters, the liberal arts, whence springs the source of religious science.' So wrote Guy de Basoches, come from distant Champagne to make pilgrimage like hundreds of his kind to the long, narrow island at the heart of Paris. At the time that he was writing, about 1190, the centre of the island was in the hands of masons and from it was rising the enormous structure of Notre-Dame, the church of Paris which had only recently acquired its status of cathedral. The king, Philip Augustus, had thrown his immense energies into the creation of a Paris that would be a fit setting for the new-risen glory of the monarchy. The filthy streets were gradually being cleansed and neatly paved: at the *louvre* — the open space near the river — a new palace was rising to match its secular pomp to that of the Cathedral. But Guy's allegory ran away with him; the only palace that philosophy had lay in the scattered houses of the masters: the Seven Sisters still dwelt at the street corners. The University was still an idea, not yet a place and would continue so for many years to come. The fact constituted a strength, in those early dangerous years when the University was struggling to free itself from the cathedral that gave it birth, from the city that sheltered it, and from the papacy that protected it. Under pressure, masters and students alike could arise and go, taking with them, in addition to the few hundreds of books, the whole vast, intangible prestige of its existence. It could even dissolve itself, bringing to a temporary halt the work of the Church.

During the eleventh century the school under the shadow of Notre-Dame had been but one of many. The young man who wanted to specialise in medicine went to Montpellier; should he want to experiment in the exciting new science of logic, he went to Chartres; at Laon, Anselm had created a college of theology which outshone the claims of Paris. But gradually, throughout that century, the wandering students, passing from Laon to Chartres to Angers, or to some obscure monastery made temporarily famous by a new teacher, would come at last to the banks of the Seine, and, crossing it by one of the two bridges, would find himself in the narrow, crowded, ill-smelling streets of the Île de la Cité. There he would seek out, or drift to one master or the other and there, as often as not he stayed. Sometime about 1100 one of these wandering students, the Breton Peter Abelard, followed this path. He sat at first under the star of the Île, William of Champeaux, then destroyed him during the course of one of those disputations which was the

106

academic equivalent of the tourney, formed his own school, attracted scholars by the hundred, blazed in brief triumph and then was himself destroyed. Abelard, branded as a heretic, forged the instrument which Aquinas was to use a century later, but what was as important was the magnetism which he had imparted to Paris.

The University that came into being some time about the year 1190 was simply the association of masters, who combined for common profit and protection as would the members of any other body. *Universitas* was a common term, applicable to a guild of tradesmen as well as to a corporation of savants. The Statutes of Montpellier made explicit the correspondence between a university of masters and a guild of craftsmen. 'If a master is attacked directly or through one of his supporters by one who is not of the school, all other masters shall bring him counsel and aid if summoned for the purpose.' The profit motive was recognised as explicitly. 'If a master be in litigation with one of his pupils about his pay, no other master shall knowingly accept the student before he has given or promised satisfaction to his former master.' Similar provisions applied to the University of Paris masters. The progress from *universitas* to University, the development from a trade guild to an immensely powerful body which challenged or supported kings and popes, was measured by the progress of rebellion from the cathedral, the body that gave it birth.

The spirit of independence which informed the University of masters was totally at variance with that absolute obedience which the Cathedral chapter expected of the thing it had created. In the person of its secretary, the chancellor, it reserved to itself the right of granting the vital licence to teach. But, as with any other trade guild, the University sought to impose conditions upon those it admitted to its ranks — even if a man were licensed by the chancellor, his fellow-masters found ways to prevent him teaching if they disapproved of him. It was a situation with all the ingredients for an explosion.

At the heart of the opposition to the chancellor were the 'artists' — those masters who taught one or other of the Seven Arts. At some time before the end of the twelfth century the four main branches of study at Notre-Dame — those of Theology, Medicine, Canon Law and Arts — were formed into distinct faculties of which that of Arts was the largest, the junior, and the most unruly. The practitioners were young men, for study of the Arts was only a prelude to the other three — 16 years of study were required before a man could profess theology. At once students and masters, of an uncertain status, ambitious and energetic, it was the artists who, forced to organise themselves in their battle against authority, were to give form to the University itself. In 1220 they crossed their Rubicon, removing themselves from the control of the Cathedral by migrating across the Seine and establishing themselves upon the left bank of the river on the Montagne Ste-Geneviève. The abbot of Ste-Geneviève, ever anxious to extend his authority at the expense of the bishop, willingly granted them the necessary licences. At about the same time, the faculty organised itself on a regional basis with the creation of the Four Nations — Norman, French, Picard and English — each with a proctor who later elected a rector for the whole faculty. The faculty of Arts thus provided a formal head for the University by the middle of the thirteenth century: the theologians, whose superior status should have made them the natural leaders of the University, were disqualified in the minds of both students and masters by the chancellor's claims to be, *ex officio*, head of the Theology faculty.

In its struggle with the Cathedral, the University had two powerful allies in the king and the pope. It was Philip Augustus who, in 1200, gave the first charter of privileges to the University, even curtailing the rights of his own Provost to do so. The charter arose out of one of the violent 'town and gown' rows which were the physical counterpart of the intellectual struggle between Cathedral and University. Philip himself was impressed by the readiness of the tonsured clerics of the University for street brawling, 'They are hardier than knights, for even armoured knights hesitate to engage in battle. These clerks, having neither hauberk nor helmet, throw themselves into the fight armed only with daggers.' A servant of one of the German students had been beaten up by a tavernkeeper; his master's compatriots in their turn descended upon the tavern and nearly killed the owner. Promptly the townspeople armed themselves, summoned the Provost who, exercising perhaps unnecessary force, managed to kill five scholars while attempting to arrest the originators of the brawl. Masters and students alike complained to the king, threatening that all lectures would be suspended, the academic life of Paris brought to a halt unless the murders were avenged. Philip Augustus went to extreme lengths to placate the offended University. The Provost and his officers were imprisoned and the principle was established that, hereafter, members of the University were exempt from the civil power.

The exemption was a privilege only too likely to be abused. The University was an ecclesiastic organisation and the power of controlling its members lay with the superior ecclesiastic body in the city — the Bishop and the Chapter of the Cathedral against whom the University was in a permanent state of rebellion. Almost 30 years after the riot of 1200, another tavern brawl precipitated another riot with the consequent deaths of more scholars. The Chapter gave the civil power a free hand in the disciplining of its rebellious child; the University promptly suspended all lectures and, that failing to gain its purpose, then formally dispersed itself for six years. Oxford and Cambridge, Rheims, Orleans and Toulouse offered hospitality to the homeless scholars and received in return an incalculable benefit from their guests. For over two years Paris was bereft of its greatest treasure; the University declined to return without adequate guarantees which would bolster the charter of Philip Augustus. It was at this point that the papacy intervened.

Throughout its early years the University had been the solicitous object of the papacy who saw in this still inchoate organisation the means to extend the power of Rome, to limit the power of the bishops, to hinder above all the dangerous and growing movement towards an independent Gallic Church. The University had stumbled into greatness, a series of accidents had attracted the leading minds of the day to set up their schools in and around the Île de la Cité, now it was becoming the intellectual forum of Europe and common sense dictated that it should be tied, if possible, to pope rather than to bishop. Innocent III had already recognised its legal existence by his approval, in 1212, of a University representative at the papal court and, further, explicitly forbade the chancellor to exact an oath of obedience from the masters. Two years later his cardinal Robert of Courson had taken a hand in the formal organisation of the University, his statute containing the first mention of the organisation's new title '*Universitas magistrorum et scholarium*'. Peter of Nemours, Bishop of Paris, promptly challenged this right of association, threatening both student and master with excommunication if they should dare form coalitions. He brought down upon

110

himself the weight of the Holy See and his chancellor was summoned to Rome to justify his actions. 'It is a shame that an officer of the bishop harms the great school of Paris and stops the flow of the great river of knowledge which, through its many branches, waters and nourishes the land of the universal Church.'

The exodus of 1229 gave the papacy incentive and opportunity to confer more privileges on the University. The title of the bull of 1231, *Parens scientiarum*, could not have deferred more to the pride of the masters: their University was the 'mother of sciences' and as such the control of the chancellor over it was to be abolished. Under these terms the University agreed to return. But the papacy was mistaken if it thought that loyalty would spring from gratitude. A generation afterwards and the University attempted to impose an oath of obedience on the teaching friars who were bound by oath only to their own Orders and to the pope. Failing, and being threatened by excommunication for their attempts, the University dissolved itself. There was little that the papacy could oppose to the ultimate weapon of suicide and the University eventually had its way, the friars taking the oath of obedience in 1318. The University had declared itself free not only of the local church which had created it but the universal Church which protected it. Benedict Gaetani, the papal legate, who as Boniface VIII was to be destroyed by France, raged against the arrogance of the University which now thought itself capable of questioning the decrees of the pontiff himself. 'You Paris masters at your desks seem to think that the world should be ruled by your reasonings. It is to us that the world is entrusted, not you.' He warned the masters that they, as clerics, were still subject to the pope, who could, if he so wished, deprive them of all offices. 'I truthfully declare to you that, rather than go back on its word, the Court of Rome would destroy the University.' A century later, during the Schism, it was the University who pronounced upon the legitimacy of popes.

Realists and Nominalists

William of Armorica, writing about 1210, speaks of Paris as already being the intellectual centre of Europe.

> Never before in any time or any part of the world, whether in Athens or in Egypt, had there been such a multitude of scholars. The reason for this must be sought not only in the admirable beauties of Paris but also in the special privileges which King Philip [Augustus] and his father before him conferred upon the scholars. In that great city the study of the *Trivium* and *Quadrivium*… were held in high esteem. But the crowd pressed with a special zeal about the chairs where Holy Scripture was taught, or where problems of theology were solved.

He was, perhaps, being unduly sanguine: for every problem of theology that was solved a dozen more were raised, breaking bodies and reputations in the process. At the time that he was writing there was a lull: both Abelard and his great opponent Bernard had been dead this last half century and another half century was to pass before Albertus Magnus and his pupil Aquinas came to hammer into a whole the sum of theology. But the strands existed to link heretic and saint, the one working still in the age of the schools, the other in that of the University.

Scholasticism was founded upon one aspect of the works of one author — the two treatises by Aristotle entitled *Categories* and *On Interpretation*. By an historical accident the study of logic embodied in these treatises was one of the few sciences to survive the wreck of the classic world; analytical minds which, in later periods, would be at work on a far greater range of sciences were, perforce, limited to this essentially ancillary study. The whole vast structure of Aristotle — particularly that part relating to ethics and the natural sciences — did not become available to Europeans until the mid-thirteenth century. His earlier commentators, unknown to themselves, were working merely upon the tip of a buried pyramid. They were not even in direct contact with the mind of the man whom they designated simply as 'The Philosopher', for both the available treatises came to them through the medium of Boethius' version. The very sentence that sparked off the long battle between 'Realists' and 'Nominalists' was itself contained in the work of a commentator upon the *Categories*, Porphyry's *Isagoge*: 'Now concerning genera and species, the questions whether they have substantial existence or are mere products of the intellect... I shall refuse to answer. These are problems of the highest importance and require more thorough investigation. '

In this manner did Porphyry avoid an almost impossible task. The questions were to receive more thorough investigation — and to excess — between the years 1100 and 1300. It seemed that all the world was chopping logic. 'Our scholars do not want to know about the structure of the earth, the virtue of the elements, the position of the stars, the nature of animals, the velocity of the wind, about trees or roots. They think they can solve the riddle of the Universe', the abbot of St-Victor complained. Compounded, it seems today, of dust and bones, the controversy was nevertheless the restating of an enduring problem of philosophy. How can the mind perceive classes of things when the senses are aware only of separate phenomena? Is 'humanity' — that which is common to all humans —

merely a term employed for semantic convenience or does it exist, in its own right, as a reality? Nominalists held that it did not, Realists held that it did. Between the two extremes were countless shades of opinion and now one, now the other belief was dominant in response to the teachings of a powerful adherent. Realism was, in general, that which was held to be embodied in orthodox teaching and its champions were also the champions of the conservative element in the Church. The universal preceded the particular and the theological implications of Realism was summed up by Anselm: 'I believe in order that I may understand.' Nominalism was to be the party of rebellion, for it held that, from observation of the particular, the universal could, by reason, be deduced. 'A doctrine is believed,' says Abelard, 'not because God has said it, but because we are convinced by reason that it is so.'

Beginning as a purely intellectual debate, the controversy very rapidly was infused with all the bitterness of religious warfare for, of its nature, it could not but seek to modify theology. Thus Berengarius of Tours was forced, by his Nominalist viewpoint, to claim that transubstantiation could only be ideal, not real. Roscelin, for the same reasons, came to the conclusion that there were, in effect, three Gods because there were no real universals, only individuals. Both Berengarius and Roscelin were forced to retract their position — two out of many casualties in the Nominalist camp. Abelard came to turn the tables upon the Realists and, in his turn, fell victim to the orthodox, in the person of St Bernard.

The long and bitter duel between Abelard and Bernard contained in it all the elements of the first growth of scholasticism. Abelard, the son of a noble Breton house, came to Paris about the year 1100. He was not then 21 years of age. He had voluntarily abandoned all that was his right as the eldest son, yielding his heritage to a younger brother. Other men had made similar renunciation for the love of God. Abelard, though intending to make his way along that ecclesiastic path which was the only route open to a scholar, was moved less by abstract love of God than positive love of learning. He entered the school of William of Champeaux, foremost champion of the Realism of the day, who had taken his position to an extreme. Abelard did not long remain content to sit in silence. With that dancing humour which, combined with a razor-sharp mind and profound learning, made him the deadliest of opponents, he forced William on to ever-more untenable grounds. William taught that individuals were mere accidents of their universal; if this is so, Abelard mocked, then all humanity must be absorbed in one individual unless each individual represented both species and genus in himself. At last the old man was driven to resign his chair at Notre-Dame, a chair which Abelard later filled for a brief period. He was to pay very dearly for that triumph: William of Champeaux was the friend of Bernard of Clairvaux.

Superficially, Bernard is easily cast for the role of dour churchman implacably intent upon suppressing freedom of thought. But the quality of his life removes him from any suspicion of a narrow, doctrinaire interpretation of the abiding mystery of existence. In his life there was something of Francis of Assisi in the love which he bore for nature; something of Catherine of Siena in his reluctant, yet inspired, participation in Church politics. His own background was not dissimilar to Abelard's, for he too was the son of a noble house and had deliberately turned his back upon its privileges. His father, a Burgundian knight, had fallen in the First Crusade and Bernard occasionally betrays the fact that the trappings of war exerted an attraction for him. At about the time that Abelard was at the peak of his triumph, newly installed in the chair of theology at Notre-Dame, Bernard joined the small, poor monastery at Cîteaux, some 12 miles from Dijon. In 1115, two years after entering the monastery, he was chosen by his abbot to found a daughter-house of Clairvaux. Bernard so drove himself that he would probably have died of his exertions and self-imposed privations had not William of Champeaux obtained from Cîteaux permission to take him under his jurisdiction. William forced him to eat, to rest his emaciated body, and so nursed him back to health. During that period, he introduced the young monk to a wide intellectual audience and gradually Bernard's reputation grew, a reputation based on great learning as well as on the purity and dedication of his life. In 1130 he was called upon to arbitrate between two rival claimants to the papal throne and his decision in favour of Innocent I eventually brought most of Europe behind that pope. Backed by the enormous prestige of this incident, Bernard began to move in on the attack on Abelard.

The 'indomitable rhinoceros' had made enemies enough with his too-flashing wit, his too-easy triumphs. There were now as many awaiting his destruction as there were those urging him on to ever-greater heights. In Bernard's eyes he stood for all that was destructive. Abelard might argue that reason was God-given, its employment not merely permitted but enjoined by the parable of the talents. To Bernard, whose whole life was devoted to the erection of a bulwark against paganism and heresy, reason was a loophole for the Devil. The method he chose to destroy Abelard was unworthy of him; it was nevertheless a necessary consequence of his belief: a virtuous man took part in disputations, not for the honour it might bring him, but in order to serve God — if he earned odium then that was unfortunate but irrelevant. In a sermon preached in Paris he attacked Abelard not by name but obliquely, in castigating all those 'professors' who appeared to be dazzled by their own wit; neither did he scruple to make a slighting reference to the tragedy of Heloise, seduced by a masterless man. Abelard retaliated by challenging Bernard to a contest on his own field. Bernard declared himself 'a stripling too unversed in logic to meet the giant practised in every kind of debate', but he accepted — having taken the precaution of preparing the ground beforehand. Abelard was the darling of the schools, the hero of the students; Bernard had behind him the solid support of the hierarchy — above all that of the pope who owed his very throne to him. The widely advertised confrontation at Sens on the Sunday after Whitsun in 1140 was a total disaster for Abelard. Whether warned beforehand or sensing from the temper of his audience that the issue was prejudged, he abruptly withdrew and appealed to Rome. The result was predictable: he was condemned as a heretic, banished to a monastery, his books burnt, his disciples offered the choice of conformity or excommunication.

But Abelard had created more than a movement which, dependent upon his personality, would die with him: he had created a system of working that, once proved, could not be dispensed with. Nothing could be more alarming to the orthodox than his work *Sic et Non*, in which he detailed the contradictory utterances of the Fathers of the Church. He intended it merely to be the starting point of a discussion but unwisely left the contradictions as they stood. His pupil, Peter Lombard, more prudently concluded each enquiry in his own *Sentences* with the orthodox solution. But from *Sic et Non* was to descend not only the *Sentences* (which, ironically, became the standard textbook on theology), but ultimately the great *Summa Theologica* of Aquinas.

But before that great monument could be raised there were fresh rebellions, fresh proscriptions. With the great flood of Aristotelian works came the flood of his Arabic commentators who had preserved him. Inimical to Christianity, they developed that aspect of his work which denied it, and many of those who used their labours fell to the lure of their teaching. Aquinas' great contribution was to fuse Aristotle totally with Christian doctrine, giving it the basis of rationalism yet keeping its summit still in faith. Yet, in the endless warfare of the University even the *Summa* would come under siege; in the fourteenth century William of Occam came from England to examine not the objects to be proved but the proofs themselves and declare them inconclusive.

Troubadours and Jongleurs

One of the most haunting images in European literature is that of the great horn-call which, blaring out over the corpses of 20,000 men in the Pass of Roncesvalles, echoes through the Pyrenees and comes at last to the ear of Charlemagne. The work of seven generations of largely unknown men went to the creation of this *Chanson de Roland*, taking as its text a few bald accounts of a minor rearguard action and producing an epic. The date of the action can be precisely pinpointed: Charlemagne was returning from an expedition to Spain and his rearguard was attacked on 15 August 778 — but the poem did not achieve its final form until about the year 1100. Over those three centuries, wandering minstrels developed a poem of some 4,000 lines in which a new race of heroes and villains was introduced to Europe: Roland himself; the friend Oliver, faithful unto death; Turpin, the wise counsellor; Ganelon, the archetypal villain whose name became so powerful a symbol of treachery that parents no longer chose it for their sons.

Humble men, speaking at first uncertainly in a new-born language, created these figures fit to stand besides those of antiquity.

The world of the *chansons de geste*, of which the *Chanson de Roland* is the pre-eminent example, was male and violent. Women found little place in it except as symbols of the home for which the hero, beset by enemies in some desert place, passionately longs. It was a world concerned almost exclusively with the past. The Crusades alone of contemporary events were considered a fitting subject to be enshrined: all other subjects were taken from that heroic period when France begins to emerge from obscurity. Violence and death, loyalty and betrayal are the leitmotives but there appears, too, the sense of springtime, of the freshness of early morning. The poet has time to turn aside from the glitter of armour, the clangour of trumpets and notice the greenness of the turf upon which the battle will be fought. There is blood upon the ground but, overhead, there is a blue sky and a gentle breeze, and after the battle there is the white road winding over the hill to be followed to the next adventure.

The *chansons* provide a vision into contemporary society of a vividness and directness equalled only by illuminated manuscripts. The method of saddling a horse, the ingredients of a meal, the way to build a castle or light a fire, the quirks of individuals — all are woven into the fabric as background to the heroes. The unknown poets knew their power and did not hesitate at blackmail to fill their purses. The annalist Lambert of Ardres bitterly attacked the author of the *Chanson d'Antioch* for his deliberate suppression of the deeds of a brave man. 'Count Arnoul performed under the walls of Antioch exploits which his great humility wished to keep concealed but, in spite of his efforts, the knowledge of his high deeds was gained by his fellow crusaders. And yet we do not see his name mentioned in the *Chanson d'Antioch*.' The reason was simple: the Count had unwisely declined to give to the troubadour a pair of scarlet hose for which he had asked and 'that is why the *Chanson* makes no mention of the Count — a hero all the more worthy because he did not stoop to ensure his fame by entertaining the sordid request of a contemptible jongleur.' Hard words, these: the jongleur could have retorted with justice that if he did not see to himself then no one else would — and what other sanction could he apply to the great but the threat of exclusion? If a man wanted a slice of immortality — why, then, he must pay the poet as he paid the priest.

In the heroic age there had been no distinction between singer and soldier. The minstrel had been an equal among his armed companions on the battlefield: away from it he boasted the additional skill of being able to turn a dramatic phrase while accompanying himself upon a harp. Before the Battle of Hastings, Taillefer sings the *Chanson de Roland*. Coming in sight of the enemy he asks, and is granted, the reward for his song — the privilege of striking the first blow in the battle. But, by the beginning of the eleventh century, the minstrel began to emerge as a separate class, at first attached to the court of a great man to sing his prowess and then, by degrees, becoming a member of an independent profession.

It was a hard and a skilled profession. The minstrel not only had to memorise scores of thousands of lines but also had to be a competent musician, an entertainer, if need be, a clown. He had to be able to juggle, to put trained animals through their paces, perform acrobatics himself — and write poetry. There was no clear-cut distinction between troubadour and jongleur, between the man who composed and the man who sang. There could be no mistaking the role of such an aristocrat as William of Aquitaine, reputed the first of the troubadours: he was the poet pure and simple, the man who spun words and perhaps made the tune for other men to publish abroad if they wished. But, at the other extreme, the humblest jongleur, while reciting an epic for the hundredth time, would not hesitate to make alterations to appeal to local patriotism or to place a dramatic moment in higher relief.

The lot of the jongleur was hard. Again and again he will turn aside from his recitations of the deeds of the great to bemoan his empty purse, his hard bed, his rumbling stomach. Rarely honoured, he yet performed a vital role in a society where villages 30 miles apart were aliens to each other. A man remained where he was born; occasionally, he might go on pilgrimage or attend one of the great fairs or a church festival. But, usually, he lived out his life within a few miles of his birthplace. The great lord and the peasant were alike caught up in a claustrophobic intimacy where every man knew his near neighbour's life down to its tiniest detail. The wandering minstrel brought a breath of a larger world.

But there was another type of singer who earned his living on the roads — a restless, usually drunken tatterdemalion still clad in the shreds of learning. On his tongue Latin remained a living language, now used to excoriate a prelate, now to wheedle a drink from an innkeeper, to flatter a prince or to seduce a girl. The 'brethren of Golias' they called themselves, and their quicksilver verse are classified in textbooks as *goliards*. There are a score of suggested derivations of the name, none precise but all pejorative: some look to the Provençal *guatidor*, a 'deceiver', as the origin, some to the Latin*gula* 'gluttony', and this is likely enough. They may even have taken the champion of the Philistines as their patron in a twisted mockery of the scholarship they had abandoned. Most of them bore the tonsure, being ordained priests, and some even had the temerity to celebrate Mass if there were no easier way to obtain food and bed — and drink. The Church provided the only path for a man who, whether from disinclination to soil his hands or a delight in the abstract, desired a career of learning. Inevitably, among the thousands of men who took the tonsure there were hundreds who had no vocation. Some continued in the comfortable life of monastery or priory: meals were at least regular and a man could always stifle discontent by reflecting on the state of the world outside. But others drifted back to that violent, exciting world. They found little enough upon which to exercise their talents. Production of clerics was considerably in excess of consumption, and few men who had broken free of the brutal cycle of labour that was the lot of most men 'in the world' had much inclination to return to it. They did, however, possess a skill gained with their tonsure — learning. They could talk of Rome and Troy, of Alexander and Caesar — above all, they could rhyme. So, having a taste for an idle life, equipped with a skill that could entertain others, they took to the roads. The nature of their wanderings took them down into the dregs of society and, very early on, respectable people recognised in them the danger they presented. In 913 the Council of Sens decreed that, should a Goliard be taken, he should be shaved, thus obliterating the tonsure which was his protection. With it, they were members of a privileged group. The hangman's noose, swinging always ready for the vagrant, could not pass that circle of shaved hair. Without it, they could be treated as the outlaws they were.

The Goliards were so identifiable a group that friends and enemies alike could refer to them as being an 'Order'. Certainly they had no formal admission to their numbers, yet the mock ceremonies and charters they produced gave an apparent shape to what was essentially a formless grouping of men with similar inclinations and talents. Versed and soaked as they were in the liturgy and rituals of the Church, they were the most accomplished parodists of formal religion. Some of these parodies were light-hearted, almost puerile essays, as in that *'Mass of the Drunkards'* where the opening versicle becomes 'I will go unto the altar of Bacchus' and, at the end, the celebrant's solemn *'Ite, missa est'* to the faithful becomes the innkeeper's *'Ite, bursa est'* to the penniless drunk. These Goliards, who had spent long hours in the study of dialectic and rhetoric, could turn their talents to clever mock-disputations such as the 'Dialogue between wine and water' where the arguments for each drink were put forward — Scholasticism standing on its head to earn a cup of wine. Their satire took a sharper edge when aimed at their late colleagues. They knew too well the weakness of their enemies, having sprung from the same source, and knew just which areas of the target were most vulnerable. Some of the satires were friendly enough. The mighty Abbot of Angers, who drank not from cups but from enormous pots, whose flesh was deemed incorruptible so pickled was it in good wine, could not have been offended by the fame offered him by some passing Goliard. Nor could that other abbot who could scarcely say Mass, so breathless was he from good living, much complain of a similar enshrinement. But sometimes the light banter of the Goliard turns into a vicious attack as in the *Gospel according to the Silver Mark* or the terrible *Passion of our Lord the Pope of the Romans according to the Gold and Silver Mark*. Here the early training of the Goliard finds effective employment: his ear, tuned by a thousand incantations of familiar verses, was able to reproduce the sacred scriptures tone for tone in a savage indictment of the simony of the papal court.

The satires and parodies of the Goliards would alone have ensured them a place in literature but even these pale beside the beauty of their lyric poetry. Learned tramps who would sooner steal than work, drink than study, they were able to evoke a haunting world that had been lost for a millennium and more — if it had ever existed outside the mind of man. More pagan than the pagans, the gods they invoked were not the terrible, vengeful gods of Olympus but the shy deities of spring and copse and meadow. In the universities, their fellows strove to erect towering *summae* which, wrought apparently in brass, crumbled with time; the brethren of Golias, tinkering with the waste products, produced verse which outlasted themselves and their world alike.

6: THE FIGHTERS

The Crusades

From the earliest days of Christianity, Palestine had been the physical goal of pious men. In vain, such as St Jerome had protested that it was as easy to reach Heaven from Britain as from Jerusalem or, as Augustine emphasised, that faith brought a man closer to Christ than the accident of place. The Christian mystery which had, above all else, localised God, gave sanctity and point to the perennial human need to wander through the world. Throughout Europe shrines of saints were achieving international fame; how much stronger, therefore, was the pull of the land where, it was taught, God Himself had sojourned for a fragment of eternity. The Cave of the Nativity and the Holy Sepulchre had both been identified as long ago as the time of the Emperor Constantine, and, over the centuries, other localities of Christ were added to the score — some spurious, most, at least in intent, genuine. The few hardy pilgrims from the north became a trickle, a stream and, by the ninth century, a flood. Regular routes were organised and, to some extent, policed. A pilgrim could even obtain a kind of passport from his bishop, with blank spaces for the insertion of his own name and object of pilgrimage.

> Be it known to you ____ that the pilgrim ____, a native of ____, has come to us and asked our advice because, incited by the great Enemy of mankind, he has killed ____. For this reason, in accordance with canon law and custom, we have pronounced that the aforesaid ____ should devote ____ years to pilgrimage. When therefore he presents himself to you pray

give him lodging, accommodation and fire, bread and water and allow him to repair at once to the Holy Places.

Armed with this or a similar document, bearing the conventional scrip and staff, the pilgrim would make his journey of 2,000 miles and more.

Jerusalem had been in Muslim hands since the seventh century, but there had long been a curious spirit of tolerance. The thousands of Christian pilgrims who flooded into the country needed to be fed, sheltered, clothed, transported, and the Muslims drew a considerable revenue from the provision of these necessities. Then, in the latter part of the ninth century, the Seljuk Turks drove out the humane Fatimite Caliphs and a new era began. Persecution and extortion took the place of tolerance and established toll: the flood of pilgrims dwindled again to a trickle and, as they returned, they brought bitter tales of the indignities to which they had been subjected. Throughout Christendom there arose a sense of indignation: it needed little to turn unarmed into armed pilgrimages — into Crusade.

But, in spite of this universal sympathy, when, in 1095, the Christians of the East appealed to their brethren in the West, only France responded. Voltaire's cutting phrase, 'they cried in Italy, but they armed themselves in France', applied to other countries than Italy. Some countries could not, others would not, do more than deplore the fate of distant Christians. Spain had her own, domestic, crusade, being locked still in the struggle with the Moor, brother to the Saracen. In England, the vast convulsions caused by William of Normandy had still not settled into the rhythm of a national life. In Germany, the call of the pope speaking for Christendom struck only dully upon ears tuned to hear the emperor. In Italy itself, Guelf and Ghibelline considered extermination of their opposites to be

126

crusade enough for any Christian. It was therefore in France alone that the cry for help received an answer, for it came at an opportune moment. The great movements of people were coming to an end and the land now was apportioned and owned. The armed knight, whose only reason for existence was war, found himself either unemployed or at war with his immediate neighbours for a scrap of land or a tenuous title. Famine was abroad, prices rising; the land seemed so overcrowded that to the deep religious impulse to free the places of God was added the older lure of new horizons. The First Crusade was to be French throughout, from inception to execution. It was a French pope Urban II, who gave it form and a French preacher, Peter the Hermit, who took it to the people; above all, it was the chivalry of France which was to descend at last upon Jerusalem, laving it in blood, creating an epic fit to stand beside those of the heroic age. The *Gesta Dei per Francos — The Deeds of God through the Franks —* was an arrogant title for a chronicler to use but it was not far from the truth. Guibert of Nogent called his own account *The Deeds of the Franks — and others — at Jerusalem* and the Saracen himself paid tribute to the truth of the statement by designating as 'Franks' all the Christians from the West throughout the three centuries of the Crusades.

A Council of the Church had been called to meet in Clermont in the November of 1095. Its primary purpose was to consider the position of the Church in France, arrange for the excommunication of the King and the Bishop of Cambrai, and only incidentally to touch upon the matter of the Crusade. But Urban saw the appeal of the Emperor Alexius as a priceless opportunity to heal the Schism between East and West, to establish, once and for all, the primacy of the Roman Pontiff over the whole Christian world, and he intended to use the Council as instrument. He was considerably helped by the presence in Clermont of refugees from Antioch and Jerusalem who lobbied energetically both before and during the Council; on the day that the pope's address was to be made the press was so great that it was given not in the cathedral but in open field to which people came in their thousands. The text of Urban's speech is lost but the tenor was reported by many who were there, so deeply impressed were they by both its sincerity and skill. Urban dwelt upon the shame that Christians should be so persecuted in the land of Christ; he offered his hearers the greatest bliss known to man — all who took the Cross and lost their lives would be assured of salvation. He seems, too, to have touched with consider-able effect upon the economic conditions of France, opening the eyes of his audience to the wider, richer life that lay overseas. The heady attraction of gaining riches while defending God swept through the enormous congregation. 'Deus vult' was the spontaneous cry and Urban took it up. 'It is indeed his will and let those words be your war-cry when you come into the presence of the enemy. You are soldiers of the Cross: wear then upon your shoulders the red badge of him who died for your salvation.' Whether Urban's suggestion was spontaneous, or calculated beforehand, the response was immediate, bringing into existence one of the great symbols of history — the red cross of the Crusader.

Urban II was both politician and priest — an honest man but an astute one, with much experience of the control of men. If the Crusade had taken the shape he intended it would have lacked something of its burning zeal — but much of the tragedy that attended it would have been averted. But once he had produced the idea of rescuing the Holy Places, it was left to another man, Peter the Hermit, to breathe life into it. Peter so took the imagination of his contemporaries that he dominates the pages of the chronicles, usurping in history Urban's role of architect of the Crusade. He was a native of Picardy, a short bald, ugly man who, with his white beard sweeping to his waist, presented the appearance of a dwarf from the romances. He was a professional hermit, emaciated, filthy beyond belief and with a quality in him that placed him in the long line of passionate reformers that Christianity has thrown up, sometimes to its cost. Peter had first-hand knowledge of conditions in the Holy Land: he is said to have abandoned a pilgrimage there to return to France in order to stir the conscience of the people and, like Urban, found the Council of Clermont a ready-made instrument. Thereafter he travelled the country, creating a massive popular movement. His appeal was directed to the little people — the peasant, the small merchant, the craftsman — and the Church backed him with its enormous power, dissolving the bonds that linked man to master so that all who answered the call were free to go. It did more: on taking the vow to go on Crusade the debtor was freed from his debt, the prisoner from his sentence. It was not a completely one-sided arrangement: the prudent usurer who stayed at home easily recouped himself for the lost debts by the granting of loans against mortgage. Lands, goods were sold or mortgaged to provide the necessities for the journey, and the man who kept his head and had a small store of capital could make a fortune.

The Council of Clermont had decreed that 15 August 1096 should be the date on which all vows should become effective. But long before that day the huge crowds which Peter had aroused began their own Crusade. It speaks much for his organising ability that, despite the absence of any kind of hierarchy, despite his own ignorance of logistics, he kept the scores of thousands together. They swept across France into Germany and at Cologne they broke into separate groups which met near Constantinople the following year. The rumour of their coming did little to comfort the Byzantines. They had asked for military aid; they received instead, it seemed, all the barbarians of the north with their wives and families — fanatical, untrained, dangerous. Alexius did what he could to help them and they moved on — plundering, slaying, torturing — eventually to fall victim to the military skill of their enemy.

Meanwhile, in France, the main body of knights was preparing to move. The names of their leaders were destined to enter European literature with the heroes of the past: Godfrey of Bouillon, Hugh of Vermandois, Robert, Duke of Normandy, who pawned his duchy to the English King, Stephen of Chartres, Baldwin of Flanders, Raymond of Toulouse. These champions of Christendom were equals — a fact which was to severely limit their value as a fighting force as each strove for the supremacy. They saw themselves as rescuing their Christian brethren yet, when at last they came to the East, it was to find that a gulf wider than that between Christian and Saracen existed between Christians of East and West. Alexius gained something from them: he prevailed upon some of them to recognise him as their overlord within his own boundaries and to restore to him all that they should win from the Turk.

The army stepped upon the shore of Asia on the Feast of Pentecost, 1097. At the Battle of Dorylaeum, the first clash with the enemy, they triumphed but it was a hollow triumph, the Turks destroying the country as they retreated to Antioch. The French wore their normal heavy armour — under a blazing Syrian sun. Sickness struck; Tancred and Baldwin fought a private war for precedence but, somehow, the French made themselves masters of Edessa where Baldwin declared himself prince in this, the first of the four Latin kingdoms. Then they moved onward to Antioch, to undertake the siege of a great city when they were already destitute and starving.

The Crusades, extending over three centuries, were to give rise to a great body of literature but in all of it there is nothing to surpass the poignancy of the *Chanson d'Antioch* which told the story of a campaign lasting a few months. Its author was Richard the Pilgrim, a retainer in the army of Robert of Flanders, who died before ever he saw Jerusalem. Two hundred years later another man took his rough work and polished it in the Provençal tongue, but the vitality of the work owed everything to the untutored man who attempted to record the horrors and the heroism he saw. He told of the rivalry between Tancred and Baldwin; of the appalling ferocity of the Christians towards both each other and the enemy; above all, he told of the privations endured which culminated in the horror of cannibalism. The French ate roots until the area was swept clean of vegetation; they then ate dogs, camels, rats until there were no more animals. They even ate their own leather harness and turned at last to Peter the Hermit for help. He upbraided them for their delicate stomachs. 'Are there not corpses of Turks in plenty? Cooked and salted they will be good to eat' — and when the supply of the freshly killed is ended, the cemeteries are still full. The casual manner in which Richard relates unimportant details increases the impression of truth and so raises the horror: the decomposed corpses are thrown into the Orontes, the edible are flayed and dried; a Turk tastes like bacon, one man jokes, while another demands a bottle of wine to wash down his meal.

But the inhabitants of Antioch were in little better shape and at length the French took it and, in an ecstasy of hatred,

131

massacred the citizens down to the last child. Bohemond made himself prince of the city and, when the French were in their turn besieged, directed the war with skill and vigour. Starving again and opposed by a large army it seemed that the Crusade would end here but the Holy Lance was fortuitously discovered, the Angels of God appeared on the hills and, from unknown depths, the French dragged the strength to assault the besiegers and destroy them. From Antioch they went on to Jerusalem, coming in sight of it just three years after they had left France. Again the terrible sequence of siege and massacre was repeated: the blood in the Mosque of Omar ran a foot deep; the streets were carpeted with severed hands and heads; the Jews were burnt alive in their own synagogues. In this manner the Christians celebrated the taking of the Holy City where Godfrey, refusing the crown, took the simple title of Advocate.

The First Crusade ended with the capture of Jerusalem but as, one by one, the great leaders died, so the menace of the Saracens increased. In 1146 the city again fell into their hands. And again Crusade was preached, Bernard of Clairvaux lending his voice to stir men to an enterprise for which he later gained bitter abuse. The host of the common people who joined the kings of Europe were moved less by the desire to free the Tomb of Christ than by reports of the sybaritic life which the meanest man could lead in the East.

> Every day our relatives and friends come over to join us, abandoning the property they possess in the West. Those who were poor in their native country have waxed rich here, by the grace of God. Those who owned only a few crowns here possess a large number of besants: to those who had merely a farm, God has given a town, for he will not suffer those who have taken the Cross to pine away in misery and distress.

The descriptions of the first Christian settlements, such as this by Foulque of Chartres, were a powerful incentive to hungry men in Europe. The purists were shocked by the ease with which the French adopted the life and customs of the decadent East, shocked too by the tolerance, and indeed affection, that sprang up between Christian and Muslim soldier. Each referred to the other by formal insults but each was aware of the quality of the other. The chronicles abound in reports of incidents similar to that experienced by Joinville after his capture. He had a tumour in his throat which prevented him drinking and his companions wept, believing him to be a dead man. 'Then one of the Saracen knights told me to be of good comfort, for he would give me somewhat to drink whereby I should be cured within two days; and this he did.' Among the party was a knight so badly wounded that he could not walk. 'An old Saracen knight would carry him, hanging from his neck, whenever the sick man's necessities so required.'

The Second Crusade went down to Palestine to defeat and death, caused as much by dissension among the leaders as by the martial skill of the Saracens. Jerusalem finally fell into the hands of Saladin, the greatest of them, ending 88 years of Christian rule. Once more the call went out but this time the response was dubious: men now were less convinced that the most direct path to virtue and riches lay through a pile of Saracen corpses. The satirist Rutebeuf spoke unambiguously for these colder souls: 'A man can do very well in his own country and obtain God without running much risk. Tell the Sultan that I don't care much for his threats. If he comes here, so much the worse for him — but I shan't go in pursuit of him.' It was for the great ones of the earth to earn glory by defence of the Holy Sepulchre for had not God granted them large incomes? For the rest, it was better to stay at home and till one's own fields.

The Castle

The great stone towers that dotted the land were the physical expressions of the nature of society and the conditions under which the people lived. Each was the centre of a tiny state, more or less independent according to the power of the baron who dwelt within it. Each had its own court, modelled on the same principle as the court of the monarch, differing only in size. Sometimes even that distinction was absent, the court of a great baron rivalling or even surpassing that of his suzerain. The Sire de Coucy maintained a permanent bodyguard of 50 knights: each of these would have, at the very least, ten retainers so that the court at Coucy numbered some 500 men, most of them of the nobility, quite apart from the numbers of court servants. These little states maintained the anarchy which allowed them to exist — in Suger's vivid words, the castles that housed them were 'disembowelling the king'. Their châtelains earned for themselves the nickname of '*hoberaux*' for, like a hawk, the baron would swoop out upon the defenceless neighbourhood, plunder those incapable of defending themselves and then retreat to his castle there to mock at all but the most resolute show of force.

The castle had developed far from its original humble origins of a wooden stronghold set upon a mound of earth, for it shared in that development of architectural skills which was producing the cathedrals. It could range in size from a simple keep surrounded by an outer wall to a city the size of Carcassonne. The principles employed in the fortifications of a city or the creation of an independent castle were the same, but, in such a city as Carcassonne, the castle was degraded into the citadel — an important, but subordinate part of the defences. The feudal castle in its characteristic form was a rural building, connected to and protecting some small town but essentially independent of it. Its architects were less intent upon the creation of a single, massive front than the creation of a series of obstacles each of which an invader would have to overcome before arriving at the heart. To this end every passageway was designed to twist and turn so that each part could be brought under fire from the embrasures that overlooked it. In staircases two or three steps could be taken out in an emergency; galleries would have gaps made into them, bridged by single planks which, kicked away, would leave an enemy marooned on the far side.

Regardless of the size of the fortifications there were certain features common to all types. Ringing the whole was a moat, sometimes dry, sometimes connected with a nearby river. Access to the outer, wooden wall of the castle was by a single drawbridge, protected by the barbican which was a fort in its own right. Inside the wooden wall and running round the whole complex was an open space, the lists, which an invader would have to cross. Each part of it was under surveillance from the walls, and the vulnerable areas — such as that before the gate — were able to draw a cross-fire from the advanced towers. The enemy, having penetrated as far as the lists, would now be faced with the necessity of either scaling the walls or undermining them: an attempt to take the main gate by storm would be almost useless. Set high up in the wall, the only access to it was by a ramp and drawbridge: behind it there would be at least two doors and a portcullis and every part of the passageway would draw the fire from at least one bowman. Beyond the gate was the outer courtyard. Here the social life of the castle was conducted and, in some castles, this courtyard was to prove the embryo of the town, for here were the ban oven and the chapel, the great hall of the baron, the public well, small houses and merchants' stalls. Beyond this was yet another wall and ditch and beyond that was the heart of the complex, the great donjon or keep.

About the year 1220 Enguerrand III, Sire de Coucy, began the reconstruction of the donjon of Coucy which, when it was completed, represented the flowering of a military art which survived long after the cannon was introduced. The House of Coucy produced a remarkable number of military adventurers who were to be found in mercenary armies throughout Europe, and from the proceeds of their international robberies they were enabled to indulge their taste for military architecture. A little town grew up under the protection of their castle and represented the transitional stage between the purely military establishment and the full-grown town. Coucy-le-château lay on the lower slopes of a hill and was connected to the castle on the crest by a formidable circuit of walls. But the dependence of the castle was guaranteed by an equally massive wall that roughly divided the complex in two. Beyond the wall and higher up on the hill was the *place d'armes*, in which were the domestic offices of the castle, and higher still was a great ditch behind which was the castle proper with the donjon towering above it.

Enguerrand's architect took advantage of the great changes in military techniques which had been made over the past half-century, changes which rendered vulnerable even that enormous structure, the Château-Gaillard, which Richard of England had built in Normandy. The donjon of the castle adopted the new circular form which considerably facilitated building: it was erected on a spiral system, scaffolding being added as the wall grew so that a continuous ramp was created up which materials could be brought. It was over 200 feet high from the bottom of the moat to its summit and some 100 feet wide. Access to the castle was by a single bridge over the moat and, once having crossed it and secured the gatehouse, the body of the castle was at the mercy of the invader. But the heart of it lay in the vast donjon which was separated even from the castle by another ditch topped by a wall, the *chemise*, over 20 feet high. A drawbridge lay across the ditch, leading into the entrance passageway which was successively defended by a portcullis, two doors and then an iron grill.

The passageway ended in an enormous circular chamber furnished with a fireplace and a deep well. In the centre of the roof was an opening which connected it with the nerve centre of the donjon, the assembly-place on the second storey. The first storey was similar in construction to the ground floor, except that a sally-port gave access to a bridge which led to the top of the *chemise*. On the second floor a wooden gallery ran around the walls about io feet above the floor. The additional floor area provided made it possible to muster the entire garrison, consisting of some 1,500 men, in this one chamber so that orders could be issued to all at the same time. The final storey was uncovered, save for the *hourds* or timber framing that protected the battlements. Each part of the donjon was designed to give support to the rest and an enemy would have to occupy every part before it could be taken.

As the donjon was the expression of the military function of the castle, so the great hall was the expression of its social role. Only the smaller barons would make one of the chambers of the donjon into his hall: usually, it was a separate structure capable of holding several hundred people at a time. Here it was that the baron sat in judgement, received the homage of his vassals and gave those enormous feasts which were at once a demonstration of his wealth and a social bond. Decoration was achieved by a startling use of polychrome picking out the shape of arches and pillars: more subtly the great tapestries introduced touches of colour as well as providing a limited form of insulation. Most ornaments had this practical as well as aesthetic value and were very largely limited to those in use on the dining tables. Goblets of gold, silver or precious stones, plates and cups of gold — these formed the treasure of the baron in a very real sense. They were the produce, as often as not, of loot, supplemented by gifts and, in an emergency, they could be sold, or melted down, and used to pay for soldiers and provisions. Their value was at least as great as the small store of coined specie that was likely to be in the treasure chest and, should the castle be sacked, they would be a prime object of the attention of the enemy.

The castle's furniture was as massive and solid as the castle itself, for it would be made by carpenters more skilled in the construction of roof-beams and drawbridges than in cabinet work. Sophisticated joints and panellings were unknown: the basic method of furniture-making was to glue thick planks together and clamp them with iron. The primitive method was sufficient for the very limited types of furniture in demand. The entire domestic furnishings of a castle housing perhaps 1,000 people would be less than that deemed sufficient for an establishment of 100 people today. The basic article was the simple coffer or *huche*: so fundamental was it that when, in the fourteenth century, a separate craft of cabinet-makers began to develop, its workers took the name of *huchiers*. In spite of the limitation imposed upon it by the fact that it opened from the top, it was a remarkably versatile piece of furniture and was used as wardrobe, linen cupboard, treasure chest; with a pallias upon it, it became a bed; it appeared in the kitchen as a bread-container; supplied with straps it was a travelling chest. Most other articles of furniture developed from it: an extension of its back and sides turned it into a *banc-à-dos*, an article similar to a church stall. The buffet began its life as a coffer in which shelves were added to the extended back and used to display costly objects and curios.

Far less ingenuity was expended on the great dining tables: these were simply planks of timber brought into the hall when required and laid on trestles. The guests sat on benches equipped with the *marchepied*, a bar designed to prevent the feet resting on the cold and possibly damp pavement of the hall. The great *chaire* was reserved for the baron: this too developed from the coffer, the back being raised to a height of six feet and the sides in proportion to provide arms. In time it became a symbol of authority not only for the baron but for the heads of the various domestic departments and was the first article upon decoration, in the form of carving, was used.

Beds were as rare as chairs: the servants slept on palliasses thrown down wherever there was space. They were of two main types, the open bed made of heavy beams with cords strung between and furnished with a tester or canopy, and the closed bed which was virtually a wooden box. They were probably comfortable enough for feather mattresses were used in abundance and, for the wealthy, linen or even silken sheets were available. Personal hygiene was at a high level, more nearly approximating the conditions in Ancient Greece than that achieved by the Renaissance. The evidence of the *chansons* suggest that the bath was almost a ritual: the hero on arrival at the castle of his host would be bathed by the baron's womenfolk and the young man's bath was part of the ceremony of knighthood.

The baron's table, though linked to the same cycle of famine and glut as was the peasant's table, was less affected by it. 'Food' and 'bread' might be synonymous but meat was the only dish deemed fitting for the nobility — and meat was obtained almost exclusively from the chase, a source denied the peasant. Pies and tarts and fish would figure on the menu of the feasts but they were intended only as fillers. Course after course would consist simply of different kinds of game, or different cuts from the same animal. Shoulder or head of boar, haunch of bear, venison, hare or rabbit served whole: these would alternate with game-birds — heron, duck, pigeon, pheasant. The farmyard capon would find a place and so too would the aristocratic swan and peacock, but all else would be provided by the hunter.

The curiously high honour in which the chase was held, an honour second only to that accorded to the tournament, was largely due to its value in inculcating military virtues. It needed courage and skill of a very high order to meet and hold the charge of a wounded and enraged boar — the same kind of courage and skill which a man might need to meet the charge of an enemy. There might be other men in the hunt but, in that last moment when the boar had chosen his target and was hurling himself towards it, a man was alone, wholly dependent upon his ability to hold the great lance firmly at the correct angle. The experience gained on horseback while pursuing a deer through rough country was likely to prove very useful during a mounted melee. The slaughtering of wild birds was less immediately applicable to military experience: no knight would wish to seem expert in the dishonourable weapon of the bow and game-birds were brought down by falcons. Falconry was a highly specialised art with its own complex vocabulary and rules of etiquette and was the badge of nobility — the earliest treatise upon it was written by the man they called Stupor Mundi, the Emperor Frederick II. The mews in which the trained falcons were kept were as important a part of the castle as were the stables, and the young nobleman learned how to handle the fierce creatures as part of his training for knighthood.

Behind the great walls of the castle a miniature world pursued its course. The lay equivalent of a monastery, it was a self-sufficient community which looked upon the outside world as an irrelevancy. Yet, even as the members of a monastery were linked to their brothers in other communities by the rules of their obedience, so the otherwise isolated worlds of the nobility were linked by the code of chivalry. It had grown from a common source side by side with feudalism but was independent of it. Feudalism was essentially linked to the owning of property whereas the humblest, poorest peasant could, in theory, be knighted by another knight. He then possessed the power to transmit, in his turn and by the same means, that virtue which had been transmitted to him. In sociological terms, chivalry was society's attempt to hold within a discipline those elements which were at once its scourge and its defence: as central authority grew stronger, so chivalry decayed, becoming a mere form. The knight was to defend the Church, defend the weak and himself remain pure according to the laws of God; even though such a high code was broken as often as it was honoured, it subjected the violent to some form of restraint.

Knighthood was, in practice, limited to the wealthy, if only because the lengthy training and equipment of a mounted soldier required considerable capital outlay. An armed horseman was not necessarily a knight, but a knight had to be a horseman — a fact recognised by the vernacular when it termed him a *chevalier* even though the Latin referred to him as a *miles*. A young man would start his training at about the age of 14 when his father would find for him a place in the court of another baron, usually his suzerain. It benefited both sides: the young man would be brought into contact with others of his class and would receive a concealed subsidy for his training; the suzerain would gain the loyalty of the rising generation. Chivalry, in spite of its exalted nature, was a craft guild like any other and, just as the apprentice craftsman was assigned to a master and went through successive stages of training, so the *damoiseau* was placed under the care of a veteran knight, becoming his shield-bearer or squire. A period of some seven years apprenticeship lay before him, an apprenticeship which covered not only the glamorous duties of a warrior but the humble duties of a valet. He stood behind his master at table, maintained his armour, groomed his horse, sharing with the professional servants of the court all the tasks necessary to maintain a fighting man in physical and psychological well-being. It was a galling experience for a youth of high family but, in rendering him an all-round expert at his trade, it would stand him in great value when he, in his turn, came to command men.

Knights were frequently created upon the field of battle but this occasion was usually limited to those who had performed signal service. It was then that the brave but landless man could hope to receive the accolade and, perhaps, lands to uphold his new dignity. The *damoiseau* received his accolade in a more studied ceremony. In the earlier period, until the end of the twelfth century, the ceremony was comparatively simple, the *parrain* or knighter simply buckling on the young man's armour and ending the ceremony with a blow, greater or less according to his nature. But, just as the Church had imposed its own oath of fealty upon the purely military right of homage, so it designed a ceremony which emphasised the religious nature of knighthood. On the night before the actual dubbing the young man, in the last few hours of his status as *damoiseau*, would watch over his arms in an all-night vigil in the chapel. At dawn he would place his arms upon the altar, dedicating them to God, and then hear Mass and receive Communion. Sometimes the Church was able to exert its spiritual power so far as to bestow the accolade at the hands of a bishop but usually this action remained in the hands of the laity. The aspirant's sponsors, one by one, would gird him with the pieces of his armour, beginning with the golden spurs of knighthood which would take the place of the silver spurs of the squire. He would receive his sword, the pre-eminent symbol of his profession, either from the suzerain or from his own father and then, when clothed completely as a man-at-arms, he received the accolade.

The code of chivalry, in emphasising the knight's duty towards the weak, implicitly included the duty of protecting women. There was nothing in the code, however, which could have produced the fantastic etiquette of the courts of love as it was practised in the twelfth century. This owed everything to the poet, not the moralist, and was a development of the softer civilisation of the south. The status of women in the north remained unchanged long after their sisters in the south had achieved a high degree of emancipation. Women's role was very largely a product of the same military and economic factors which shaped the land into hundreds of petty states. The *chansons* speak of her only as a passive, if vital, instrument in the transmission of fiefs. There will be conventional salutes to her beauty and virtue; she may be called upon to play a dramatic part in the hero's adventures but, until the development of the poetry of courtesy, her major role was to be bestowed upon the hero — and with her, all her lands. It is for these that the hero fights and endures privations, not for some abstract idea of sexual love or honour. The poets of the *chansons de geste* reflected their society accurately enough: the true object of a man's love should be his lord and he would dispose of his daughter or accept a wife according to his lord's behest. In practice, that love might be pure self-interest but it did not affect the truth of the proposition that all benefit came from the lord — including the benefit of possessing a wife's property. By the twelfth century a woman's right to inherit was legally recognised, whether that right consisted in following her husband's trade as cobbler or inheriting hundreds of acres of land and the wealth that went with it. But the parent or husband from whom she inherited those lands had, in their turn, been enfeoffed with them by the suzerain for military purposes; it was therefore of paramount importance to him to ensure that they remained in hands loyal to him.

The problem was sometimes avoided by betrothing the girl at an early age to a suitable man: the legal age was deemed to be 12 years old for a woman and 15 for a man, but the betrothal of children at a much younger age was a commonplace, the oaths then sworn being binding until supplanted by the marriage oaths. In the absence of an adult male in the family, the bestowal of an orphan girl or of a widow fell to the suzerain. Feudal theory required no consent on the part of the woman — but the religious ceremony which was indispensable to the marriage did demand her explicit consent. It was therefore entirely possible for a woman to thwart the wishes of her suzerain and either refuse a marriage advantageous to him or actually take an unsuitable man in marriage. It was possible — but it required an exceptionally strong-minded woman to withstand the moral and physical coercion which would be exerted upon her. She was not safe even if enclosed in the theoretically indissolvable bond of matrimony. Marriage between relatives as distant as the seventh degree was forbidden — a prohibition inevitably transgressed either wittingly or unwittingly in the close-knit society of the nobility. It was simple enough to establish such an affinity between husband and wife and declare the marriage void if politics so demanded.

But though a passive role was all that was demanded of her in theory, in practice a woman of the nobility was able to make her influence felt over a wide field. During the frequent absences of her husband on campaign or, particularly, on a crusade which could last for years, the defence of the castle fell to the woman. It was no sinecure: most of her husband's vassals would have gone with him and she would have to be prepared to repel an attack with inferior material. She would need to be versed in administrative ability to a greater or less degree, depending upon the size of the fief. When St Louis was away on crusade, the Seneschal of Carcassonne thought it worthwhile to furnish the queen with a minutely technical account of the siege of the city. Doubtless he thought it prudent to ensure that the king would eventually receive his own account of the action, but he also expected the queen's assistance in a purely military matter. The woman who actually took the field in armour was uncommon but by no means rare. The Countess of Harcourt got together a mercenary troop and set out to avenge the judicial murder of her husband making herself an intolerable nuisance in Provence. Blanche of Navarre led her armies in person during a dynastic war and the sisters of Philip Augustus actually went on crusade, leading an independent force. In the field of learning, and in particular in

145

literature, women not merely held their own but became patrons of new forms. In the south the new lyric poetry was intended not for the roistering hall of the baron but the chamber of the lady and, in singing the praises of courtesy, was to exert a profound influence on the standards of the court.

The Battlefield

War was continuous, the normal state in which society existed. The Church recognised the fact and attempted to restrain what it could not abolish by the well-meaning but hopeless 'Truce of God'. At first concerned to protect the property and lives of its own servitors, it extended the concept to include not merely protected objects but protected days. The Sabbath was sacred and therefore those who swore to observe the Truce agreed to cease fighting on Saturday evening and start again on Monday. The limited success encouraged the attempt to extend it. Each day of the week could be shown to have sacred associations: Saturday was devoted to the Virgin, Friday to the Crucifixion, Thursday to the Ascension. But the very comprehensiveness of the Truce defeated its own object for it presented to a class of people, whose whole existence was geared to war, the inescapable choice of breaking the Truce or living in perpetual peace. And peace, for most, was not merely a period of unemployment but the absence of all that which made life worth living. Bertrand de Born spoke for all such when he lamented a brief truce between Philip Augustus and Richard of England as a time when valour and bravery were dead, when castles stood as empty shells. Dante put him in hell, among the sowers of discords, where he carried his head in his hands to symbolise the manner in which he separated fathers from sons. But Bertrand spoke with the authentic voice of his class, a savage exultation at the sight of spilt blood, shattered limbs, falling towers. His gift as a poet enabled him to fuse the worlds of the butcher and the artist: the flutter of gay pennons on spears sticking out of dead bodies; the writhing of a mortally wounded man on green turf; the rich colour of blood as it coursed over steel; the rumble and dust of a collapsing wall — all these he caught in unforgettable verse which no young man could hear and not be touched. In war alone was a man whole.

Bertrand's poems provided the inarticulate with the philosophy of war; the economy of war was readily apparent to the meanest intellect. Each man's land yielded only a limited amount of wealth; to augment it, he must seize that of his neighbours and, as a natural corollary, be prepared to defend his own. The great dynastic wars that washed over the land from the fourteenth century onwards were no more destructive than the endless, petty struggles between vassal and lord, vassal and vassal, that marked the centuries before. The increased power of that central authority represented by the monarch tended to be neutralised by the increased ability of the castle to withstand siege. The weaker barons deferred to him but the stronger retained their position. And even should there be peace between members of the same class, there was no peace for the class below them. The peasant and his goods were the object of most local wars. In a pact proposed by the Bishop of Beauvais, peasants are precisely equated with animals: 'I shall seize neither oxen, nor cattle, nor other beast of burden; nor shall I seize either male or female peasant or their goods.' On his deathbed the Count of Roussillon openly admitted that the greater part of his revenue came from banditry and he desired that compensation should be made from his estate to the villagers in the hamlets near his castle.

The existence of the castle encouraged the concept of war as a test of courage between individuals. No matter how great the force brought on to the field, no matter how crushing the defeat inflicted in open battle, a war could only be deemed to be concluded when the castle of the enemy was captured and its pennon hurled into the moat. The knights in battle could therefore afford the luxury of fighting with weapons whose design scarcely changed over centuries, leaving innovations to the engineers of siegecraft. The development of projectile weapons of great power and range was matched by an increasing sophistication of defence and both were the direct result of the experience gained during the Crusades. In the century following the First Crusade, the basic shape of the castle changed from the single, square tower to the principle of the concentric castle where an invader would have to fight through successive rings of defence. On the opposing side the besiegers added two new weapons, the Turkish *petraria* and the terrible Greek fire, to the engines that had come down from antiquity, the movable castle, the 'cat' and the ram.

The central task of an attacking force was to make a breach in the wall through which fighting men could be introduced. There were three methods at its disposal: the use of the long-range projectile, the close-range ram, and the miner. The *petraria*, or trebuchet, provided an extremely efficient engine for the hurling of projectiles. Unlike the older weapons of the class which worked on the principle of torsion, the *petraria* introduced in the early thirteenth century worked by counterpoises. A long beam, thinner at one end than at the other, was balanced on a pivot supported on uprights. A heavy weight was attached to the thicker and shorter end and the other was pulled to the ground and secured by a catch. In some models a basin for the projectile was fastened to the thinner end, but others employed a sling. When the catch was released the weight would fall and the arm of the *petraria* would whip upwards and forwards, casting the projectile in a parabolic curve. The use of a sling increased the whipping action and doubled the range of the projectile. In 1850 Louis Napoleon constructed one of these engines as an experiment and it gave an impressive performance. The beam employed was nearly 34 feet long, the counterpoise weight was 9,900 lb. and a 24-lb. weight was hurled a distance of 191 yards.

Trebuchet or *petraria* were used generally to hurl crushing weights but containers of Greek fire were included amongst the ammunition, with terrible effect on the defenders. It was composed of a mixture of sulphur, pitch, nitre and petroleum boiled together. Once it had ignited, it could be put out only with sand or wine and, because the medium was a liquid, the fire would spread very rapidly into inaccessible places. But its psychological value was probably as great as its destructive qualities. The Sire de Joinville, a brave man and a veteran soldier, confessed himself appalled when he first came under fire. The attack was made at night and

> it was the most horrible thing I ever saw in my life. It made such a noise in its coming as if it were a thunderbolt falling from heaven, and it seemed to me like a great dragon flying in the air and showed so great a light that in our lines it was as light as day, so great a flame was there.

An assault at close quarters employed the cat, a kind of movable shed which was propelled very slowly and jerkily by means of rollers worked from inside. An eye-witness at the siege of Toulouse vividly described its curious motion as 'advancing with short leaps, like the sparrow-hawk when it hunts down small birds'. The cat would be thickly covered with green hides as a protection from fire dropped from the walls, and ran on boards which were moved from rear to front as it progressed. Faggots would be dropped from its interior into the moat, providing a path for it to move along. As soon as the wall was reached, the miners or the operators of the battering ram would take over. At Toulouse there was a lively period when the attackers employed rammers and miners in quick succession on the same stretch of wall. The wall was beginning to give way under the strokes of the great wheeled ram when the defenders managed to drop a noose over its head and deflect it. Miners then took over, working in an alcove which protected them from missiles from above. The defenders therefore

> sewed up, mingled together in a cloth, fire, sulphur and flax, which they let down at the end of a chain alongside the wall. And when the fire took, and the sulphur melted, the flame and smell choked the pioneers to such a degree that none of them could remain.

At the siege of Toulouse, the army of Simon de Montfort had actually forced their way into the city but had been beaten back by the combined efforts of the inhabitants — knights, burgers, workmen fighting shoulder to shoulder in the narrow streets which neutralised the superior arms of the professional soldiers. When de Montfort furiously demanded the reason for the retreat, his brother, who had been in command of the operation, voiced the dislike of all knights for siege work: 'By the fealty I owe you, not a man among us is so brave but, when they hunted us out through the gates, he would have preferred a pitched battle.' The siege might be strategically necessary and provide much booty but the knight came into his own only on the field of battle when he strove with his equals.

Mail, the basic constituent of a knight's armour, had been perfected by the end of the eleventh century and thereafter changed only in detail until it was supplanted by plate armour in the fourteenth century. The main garment was the hauberk, or shirt of mail complete with hood, consisting of steel links knitted into double or even treble layers. It was slashed at front and back to facilitate riding, and hung down as far as the knees. Leggings of mail were later attached and these, together with mail mittens ensured that, when the hood was up, every part of the body was protected except for the face. The hood was padded with fabric and when in position resembled a balaclava helmet. Quilting was introduced as an added protection in the twelfth century, the gambeson worn beneath mail being an adaptation of a Saracenic garment quilted with cotton. The helmet, worn over the hood and laced at the base, was the first article to undergo major changes. Originally a simple steel cap with a nasal guard, by the late twelfth century it had developed into the pot-helm, a massive structure which was supported on the shoulders like a modern diving helmet. Covering the entire head, it effectively concealed the identity of the wearer and it became customary to wear a device upon the crown which would assist identification. The complex art of the herald developed from this practical necessity, the surcoat and shield being the obvious places upon which to emblazon coats-of-arms. As leg protection increased, the enormous kite-shaped shield of the earlier period gradually shrank to a small, triangular object which could be easily manipulated.

Lance and sword provided the knight's offensive armament. The 8-foot long lance of ash — which increased to 15 feet by the fourteenth century — was the weapon of the knight as a unit of attack: the sword was the expression of his own individuality and achieved a mystic significance. A wealthy man's sword was ornamented with precious stones; it was blessed and had its own name and was cherished throughout its owner's life. The lance was merely a tool of war — an expendable weapon whose shaft rarely outlasted a single battle. Carried at the slope on the right shoulder while on the march, it was brought to a vertical position, its butt resting on the right-hand stirrup, immediately before action when it was lowered to a horizontal position. Watchers in the English lines at Agincourt saw what appeared to be a shimmer of light pass along the front rank of the French horse as the lances were lowered in unison. In tournament and in the charge against other knights, the lance was used to transmit the shock of attack: its less glamorous and probably more useful purpose was to pick off the infantry of the enemy. The gay pennons fluttering just below the metal head had a practical purpose — they prevented the lance from entering too far into the body of an unarmoured man.

The use of mail placed the two requirements of armour, protection and flexibility, in rough equilibrium. But gradually flexibility began to be sacrificed in favour of increased protection and pieces of plate metal were attached to the more vulnerable parts of the body. The massive pot-helm was followed by plate protection for shins, elbows, knees and breast, the parts at first attached independently but later linked together so that a complete metal shell was formed. The knight as a towering mass of metal on a metal-clad mount was almost invulnerable — but he had exchanged freedom of movement for defence and even this failed him if he were unhorsed and fatigued. The humiliation at Agincourt, when unarmoured English archers with their mallets hammered the life out of the prostrate knights, was the inevitable end of the process.

Agincourt, too, was the end of a way of life. The English had long before grasped the fact that war now was no longer the sport of nobles but an extension of politics. The individual

English knight might still retain his social contempt for the bowman, but the English King, who desired victory, not empty honour, made sure that this vital weapon was adequately represented in his army. The value of the common soldier being recognised, with a consequent increase of his numbers and his loyalty ensured by pay, overall control was far more easily maintained. Edward brought back generalship into European wars. The feudal army was essentially an army of independent groups, gathered together for a limited period. Each baron might owe loyalty to the lord above him and so, ultimately, to the suzerain, but feudal loyalty was not necessarily the same as military obedience. Phillip's attempt to impose discipline at Crécy was totally ineffectual. According to Froissart:

> The King's orders were soon passed round among his lords but none of them would turn back, for each wished to be first in the field. The van would not retire because they had got so far to the front, but those behind kept riding forward and would not stop, saying that they would get as far to the front as their fellows, and that from mere pride and jealousy.

The mad, but characteristic, action of the Duke of Alençon in riding down the retreating Genoese bowmen turned the front line into a churning chaos out of which individual knights struggled as best they could. And meanwhile, in ominous stillness, the English archers, members of the despised commonality, waited the coming of the noble victims.

During the next generation a new class of soldier appeared, professionals such as Bertrand du Guesclin, sprung from obscure origins, who treated war as the English did. But it required the holocaust of Agincourt to teach the nobility its lesson. Before the clash the Constable of France, theoretically the commanding officer, had attempted to impose a sensible battle plan which would have turned upon the English the defensive tactics they had introduced. He was not so much overruled as ignored, his social equals and superiors forcing forward their concept of war as an instrument of glory, not of policy. They fought well but died shamefully, 4,500 of them sacrificed to an ideal that had died a century before.

BIBLIOGRAPHY

INTRODUCTION — THE SHAPING OF FRANCE
FURTHER READING

F. Funck Brentano, *The Middle Ages* (tr. E. O'Neill), 1922

C. Guignebert, *Short History of the French People* (tr. F. G. Richmond), 1930

C. H. Haskins, *The Renaissance of the Twelfth Century*, 1927

E. Lavisse, ed., *Histoire de France*, 1901-2

A. Luchaire, *Social France at the time of Philip Augustus* (tr. E. B. Krehbiel), 1912

C. McEvedy, *The Penguin Atlas of Medieval History*,

A. Tilley, ed., *Medieval France*, 1922

1: RURAL SOCIETY
FURTHER READING

Philippe de Beaumanoir, *Les Coutumes du Beauvoisis*, 1842

M. Bloch, *Feudal Society* (tr. L. A. Manyon), 1961

J. Calmette, *La Societe Feodale*, 1947

G. G. Coulton, *The Medieval Village*, 1925

L. Delisle, *Etudes sur la Condition de la Classe Agricole en Normandie au Moyen Age*, 1851

2: URBAN SOCIETY
FURTHER READING

E. Levasseur, *Histoire des Classes Ouvrières et de l'Industrie en France avant 1789*, 1900

Le Livre des Métiers d'Étienne Boileau, 1879

A. Luchair, *Les Communes Françaises*, 1890

M. Saint-Leon, *Histoire de Corporations de Métiers depuis leurs Origines jusqu'en 1791*, 1909

3: THE CONTEMPORARY WORLD
FURTHER READING
M. R. James, *The Bestiary*, 1928

C. Langlois, *La Connaissance de la Nature et du Monde*, 1927

R. L. Poole, *Illustrations of Medieval Thought*, 1920

J. A. MacCulloch, *Medieval Faith and Fable*, 1932

4: ART AND ARCHITECTURE
FURTHER READING
H. Arnold, *Stained Glass of the Middle Ages in France and England*, 1955

J. Fitchen, *The Construction of Gothic Cathedrals*, 1961

E. and M. Marriage, *The Sculptures of Chartres Cathedral*, 1909

J. H. Middleton, *Illuminated Manuscripts in Classical and Medieval Times*, 1892

E. Panofsky, *Abbot Suger on the Abbey Church of Saint-Denis and its Treasures*, 1946

5: EDUCATION AND LEARNING
FURTHER READING
P. Aries, *Centuries of Childhood* (tr. R. Baldick), 1962

E. Faral, *Les Jongleurs en France au Moyen Age*, 1910

H. Rashdall, *The Universities of Europe in the Middle Ages*, 1936

A. F. Thery, *Histoire de P Education en France*, 1858

H. Waddell, *The Wandering Scholars*, 1932

6: THE FIGHTERS
FURTHER READING
L. Gautier, *Chivalry* (tr. D. C. Dunning), 1965

C. Oman, *A History of the Art of War in the Middle Ages*, 1924
S. Runciman, *A History of the Crusades*, 1951
E. E. Viollet-le-Duc, *Military Architecture*, 1897

A NOTE TO THE READER

If you have enjoyed this book enough to leave a review on **Amazon** and **Goodreads**, then we would be truly grateful.
The Estate of E.R. Chamberlin

Sapere Books is an exciting new publisher of brilliant fiction and popular history.

To find out more about our latest releases and our monthly bargain books visit our website:
saperebooks.com

Printed in Great Britain
by Amazon

19287291R00092